Books by Lauren Brown
Weeds in Winter
Grasses

Grasses

An Identification Guide

Houghton Mifflin Company   Boston 1979

PETERSON NATURE LIBRARY

Grasses

An Identification Guide

Written & Illustrated
by Lauren Brown

Brown, Lauren.
     Grasses, an identification guide.

     Bibliography: p.
     Includes index.
          1. Grasses — Northeastern States — Identification.
     I. Title.
     QK495.G74B77   584'.9'0974   78-24545
     ISBN 0-395-27624-1

Printed in the United States of America
v 10 9 8 7 6 5 4 3 2 1

Acknowledgements

My first debt is to Sterling E. Parker, an incredible old naturalist of Woodbury, Connecticut. Mr. Parker first taught me how to identify grasses and without his help I never could have started. Going to visit him and his wife was a real pleasure, for he knows everything about the outdoors and the visits always included delicious home-made, home-grown meals. Stephen Collins, of Southern Connecticut State College, gave me a lot of encouragement in the early stages, as did Alfred E. Schuyler of the Academy of Natural Sciences of Philadelphia. Mr. Schuyler also gave me much helpful advice in the later stages of the book.

Several people read the preliminary manuscript and made comments. These include Bill Tans of the Wisconsin Department of Natural Resources, Neil Hotchkiss, author of *Common Marsh, Underwater and Floating-leaved Plants of the United States and Canada*, Chris Campbell of Harvard University, and Claude Phillips, author of *Weeds of the Northeast*.

I received a great deal of help in identification from A. W. H. Damman of the University of Connecticut, who was very generous with his time. Another person who helped me out in the field was Robert Meyer of Whitehouse Station, N.J. I spent a bleak, rainy, fall afternoon in the Albany sand plains with the late Stanley J. Smith. All I remember of that afternoon is rain, trash, and everywhere the red of *Cycloloma atriplicifolia*. I learned a tremendous amount and consider myself lucky to have had this opportunity.

I got to know two people better through this project and am glad of it: Don Stokes and Jerry Jenkins. Don and I spent good times in the field. He showed me how a perceptive nonbotanist sees grasses and gave me a lot of encouragement. Jerry read the entire final manuscript with a fine-toothed comb, on extremely short notice, and I am very grateful to him.

The final manuscript was also read by my friends Lloyd Irland, Elizabeth Johnson, Ellen Baum and Jeff Fischer. Joe Pratt supplied the information on *Livia maculipennis* and Gary Wolfe gave me a metric conversion chart.

The person who helped the most probably doesn't realize it. This is Jim Rodman of Yale University. He, first, gave me a job on which to support myself while I was writing the book, and second, gave me unlimited access to the Yale herbarium. The resources of the herbarium were extremely valuable.

I had no patient wife sitting at home typing. This was done instead by Martha Achilles, a professional who nevertheless went out of her way to accommodate my deadlines and was always cheerful.

At Houghton Mifflin production went smoothly from start to finish due to the competent editing of Lisa Gray Fisher. I have met few people who are so thorough, patient and pleasant. The book was designed by Carol Goldenberg and visiting Lisa and Carol was always fun. Jim Thompson helped me through the initial contract stages and Anita McClellan was my first of many friendly contacts there.

Table of Contents

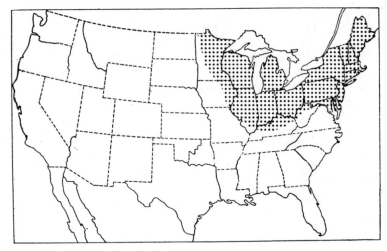

Map of area covered by this book

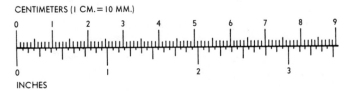

Comparison of millimeter and inch scales.

Introduction

Vast areas of the earth are covered by grass. Of the fifteen major crops that stand between us and starvation, ten are grasses. No matter where you live in the United States, you would be hard put to walk outside your door and not find grasses within a very short distance. Grasses are immensely common and immensely important.

Yet few people — even those who are passionately interested in nature — take the trouble to learn the names of grasses. Enthusiasts who will travel hundreds of miles to look at "wildflowers" ignore the grasses in their own backyard (even though they are technically also wildflowers). Most popular wildflower identification guides — even the most comprehensive — do not deal with grasses at all.

Misconceptions about grasses abound. "They have no flowers!" one hears. This is not true. Grasses do have flowers, just as roses and daisies have flowers; the only difference is that they are small and inconspicuous, and differ slightly in structure. "They have no color!" This is not true if you just start looking. "They all look alike!" Also not true if you look.

Once you start to notice various kinds of grasses, you will probably want names to attach to them. If you have ever tried to identify grasses from most existing books, you have probably met with intense frustration. The identification systems in these books are based mainly on the characteristics of the individual flower. There are valid scientific reasons for such a system, but the flowers are so small that it is hard to see the necessary characteristics without a hand lens or a microscope. Furthermore, a whole terminology has been developed for grasses that does not apply to other flowers and is not exactly self-explanatory. To identify grasses with existing technical manuals requires a fair amount of botanical knowledge, an endless amount of patience, and luck.

For the common grasses that are all around us, such technical identification methods are not necessary. My father, who is a very intelligent man but does not know plants, came to me one day after working around the house and said, "I just noticed ten different kinds of grasses in the last half hour! What are they?" My father did not notice glumes, lemmas, and paleas — the technical terms for the different parts of the grass flower. Rather he noticed obvious characteristics — general shape, color, and texture. Identification in this book is based on these characteristics. The book is written for the lay person, and requires no specialized botanical knowledge.

Two other large groups of plants are easily mistaken for grasses — the sedges and the rushes. Common sedges and rushes are also included in this book, as well as a few other plants that could easily be mistaken for grasses. There is no need to know the differences between these groups in order to identify them from this book.

What is a grass? A grass is a plant in the Grass family. A family is a large group of plants considered by botanists to have similar characteristics. To botanists, the Grass family is the Gramineae (or in some books the Poaceae). Plants in the Grass family have narrow leaves with parallel veins and small inconspicuous flowers. The stems are mainly hollow except at the point where the leaf is attached (the node). The stems have joints — easily visible bulges — where the leaves are attached. If you know the slightest bit of 1960s counterculture jargon, just remember that grass means joint and you will never forget how to recognize a grass. Grass stems are usually round. The base of the leaf wraps around the stem in a structure called the sheath (see p. 226). The sheath is open at least part way down. The flowers are arranged on the stalks in two rows. The flowers have a specialized structure as shown in the illustration.

Between each lemma and palea are the male and female flower parts—stamens and pistil.

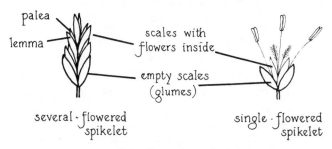

several-flowered spikelet

single-flowered spikelet

Grass flower cluster (spikelet);
flowers arranged in two rows.

Grasses are of vast ecological and economic importance, and they move around the earth easily with man. One quarter of the grass species in the northeastern United States, and some of the most common, are not native to this continent but have arrived since the European settlement. Grasses are important as crops and as weeds.

Sedges, on the other hand, have mainly solid stems, often triangular. (You may have heard that "sedges have edges." This is true for many, though not all, members of the family.) Sedge stems have no joints and the sheaths are closed. The flowers are arranged spirally on the stalk and have a slightly different structure from the grass flowers, as illustrated. Sedges tend to grow in wetter, colder areas than grasses.

scales with flowers inside

Sedge spikelets do not have the two empty scales (glumes) at the base, nor do they have lemmas and paleas. Each flower is enclosed by just one scale.

Sedge flower cluster (spikelet);
flowers spirally arranged.

For some reason, sedges have not attained the economic importance of grasses. Perhaps because they are not as often used by man they tend to migrate less than grasses, and few sedges become weeds. Of the sedge species in the northeastern United States, only four percent are alien.

Rushes are a much smaller family than the grasses or sedges, and they also have not assumed great economic importance. Like grasses and sedges, they have linear leaves with parallel veins and inconspicuous flowers. The flowers, however, are more like the flower of a lily than that of a grass or a sedge. They have three petals and three sepals, arranged in a circle, but they are small and usually dully colored so that you probably never noticed the similarity (see illustration). The fruit in the Rush family is a small three-parted capsule that usually stays on the plant for most of the season. It is filled with tiny seeds. The stems in the Rush family are either solid or hollow and the plants tend to grow in cool, wet areas.

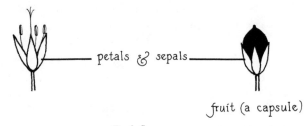

petals & sepals

fruit (a capsule)

Rush flower.

Why Bother with Grasses?

Grasses cover almost one third of the area of the earth. They cover approximately one half the area of the United States. The Grass family has the third largest number of species in the world, exceeded only by the Orchid and the Daisy families. Of the vascular plants, grasses can be found at the outermost extremes of climatic conditions; there they are surpassed only by lichens and algae. And the fruit of the Grass family — the grain — is a concentrated source of protein, carbohydrates, and minerals. Being dry, it is easy to store and transport and thus it has become a major food source for humans.

The following grains come from plants in the Grass family: Wheat, Rye, Corn, Rice, Oats, Barley, Sorghum, and Millet. The green leafy parts of grass, which we cannot digest, can be eaten by cows and other animals, so that even if you eat nothing but hamburger, you are still eating grass. If you eat sugar, you are eating another product of the Grass family, the sugarcane plant. And in the Far East, another grass, bamboo, is used for everything from food to a construction material.

Why are grasses so successful in covering such large areas of the globe? In the grasslands of the world, the main obstacles to a plant's survival are drought (dry, windy climates), fire, and grazing by animals (although the animals and the grass probably evolved there simultaneously). Grasses have several features that help them to withstand these stresses and enable them to dominate large areas.

In most plants, the tissue responsible for growth and cell division is located at the tip of the leaf or the shoot. This means that if the leaf or shoot is clipped, it will not grow back (although the plant might send out new side branches from elsewhere). In the grasses, and in a few other plants, the growth tissue is located toward the base of the leaf or the shoot. This means that if the shoot gets cropped, burned, or grazed, it can grow back from the base. The grass plant can also send out side shoots called tillers, which grow from buds near the ground. You may have noticed that many grasses (called bunch grasses) grow in clumps. This is because of tiller production. Many perennial grasses have rhizomes or stolons, horizontal stems that crawl either above or below ground and send out new shoots and roots. These grasses usually spread in such a way that the distance between the shoots is very short, and the plant forms a dense mat. These species are called sod formers and are good for use in lawns. Once a dense sod is formed, it is hard for other species to penetrate it.

Lastly, one of the most extraordinary features of grass growth is the root system. The stems and leaves that you see above ground are a small fraction of the total living weight of the plant. Sometimes as much as ninety percent of the weight of the grass plants is in the roots. This concentration of starch and energy below ground helps grasses to survive grazing and burning, and it reduces water loss. Most grasslands are in relatively dry climates where plants lose considerable amounts of water through evaporation. If most of the plant tissue were above ground, the plant would lose too much water to survive. The statistics on grass roots are staggering. In one famous study, a researcher measured all the roots of a four-month-old Rye plant grown in a greenhouse and found their total combined length to be 387 miles. The root system of the grasses is extensively branched, so that it makes the most efficient use possible of the available soil space. Such a dense root system also discourages competition by other species. Sometimes on the plains you will see patches of grass interspersed with patches of bare ground. You might wonder why nothing is growing on the bare ground, but it is because the grass roots underneath have formed such a dense network that nothing else can penetrate.

Ecology of American Grasslands

In many parts of the United States (or the world) you can find grasses growing in more or less uninterrupted stretches — meadows, pastures, prairies, plains, cultivated fields, salt marshes, and lawns. In many of these places in the northeastern United States, these grasslands would quickly turn to forest if they were not mowed periodically. (The only self-maintaining grassland in the Northeast is the salt marsh along the coast.) The "natural" vegetation of the eastern part of the country is forest; that is the vegetation that will grow and maintain itself if left alone. The "natural" vegetation of most of the Midwest is presumably grassland. When American settlers reached the prairie in Illinois, they were awed and baffled. One wrote in 1824, "I am at a loss to account for the formation of these extraordinary meadows, and all the theories I have read upon

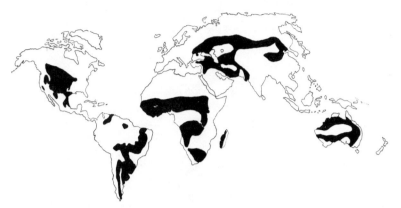

Adapted from the *Encyclopedia Brittanica* article, "Grasslands," 15th edition, volume 8.

the subject appear to me very unsatisfactory." That same sentence could be written now, for scholars are still trying to explain why grasses grow where they do and trees do not. The answer is not simple.

Trees need more water than grasses for three reasons. First they are bigger. Second, a much greater portion of their living tissue is above ground and thus subject to evaporation. Third, they need water over a longer portion of the growing season because they need to produce woody tissue as well as leaves and flowers. Most grasses do most of their growing in brief periods. Their flowering shoots are only alive and green for a short time; then they are brown and dead though still on the plant.

The grasslands of central North America are generally divided into three groups as shown on the map on p. 8. From west to east, they are the short-grass prairie, the mixed-grass prairie, and the tall-grass prairie. The boundaries of these three regions are extremely fluid, subject to change over time and subject to dispute among scholars.

As its name implies, the short-grass prairie is dominated by short grasses a few inches in height. Two of the most common species are Buffalo Grass (*Buchloë dactyloides*) and Blue Grama Grass (*Bouteloua gracilis*). The short-grass prairie is basically

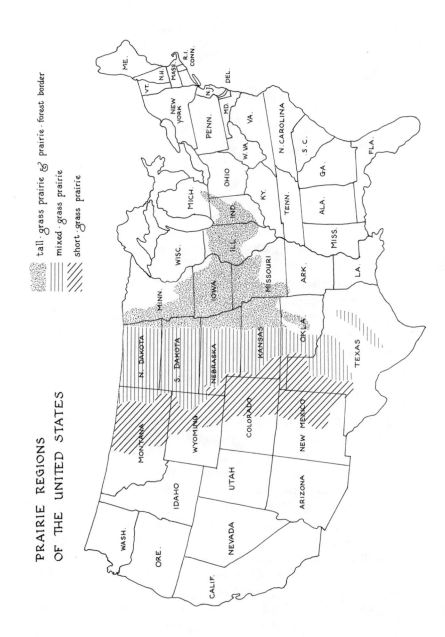

PRAIRIE REGIONS
OF THE UNITED STATES

tall · grass prairie *&* prairie · forest border
mixed · grass prairie
short · grass prairie

the same formation as the Russian steppe and could be correctly called a steppe. Most often the American short-grass prairie is referred to as the Great Plains. This is ranching country, since the most dependable use of the short-grass prairie is livestock grazing. Wheat has been grown there but rainfall is too irregular to assure a steady crop.

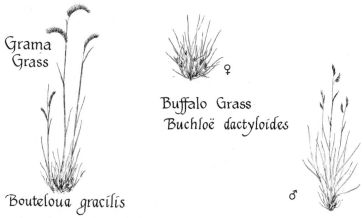

Grama Grass

Buffalo Grass
Buchloë dactyloides

♀

♂

Bouteloua gracilis

Adapted from A. S. Hitchcock's *Manual of Grasses of the United States*, 2nd edition.

For the short-grass prairie, the answer to why there are no trees is probably pretty simple: not enough rain. As moist air comes off the Pacific Ocean it is intercepted by the Rocky Mountains, forming eastward what is called a rain shadow. Rainfall in the Great Plains is about ten to fifteen inches per year — too little for tree growth. It is irregular through the season and varies greatly from one year to the next. Rain does not penetrate as far as the water table and there is a layer of subsoil that is permanently dry.

East of the short-grass prairie is the mixed-grass prairie, an area of transition between the short-grass and the tall-grass prairies, both in terms of rainfall and species composition. The grasses there grow about two to four feet tall and include Little Bluestem (*Andropogon scoparius*), June Grass (*Koeleria cristata*), Needle Grass (*Stipa spartea*), and Western Wheatgrass (*Agropyron smithii*), as well as species of the short- and tall-grass prairies. The boundaries of the mixed-grass prairie are by no means stable. In the course of a few dry years mid-grasses like Little Bluestem die out and the short grasses take over. Then over a few wet years the Little Bluestem will come back in. Much of the mixed prairie has been overgrazed and the grazing pressure has caused the mid-grasses to give way to short grasses. If grazing pressure were relaxed, then the mid-grasses could come back. The area of the mixed-grass prairie corresponds roughly to what is now called the Wheat Belt.

The area that most defies simple explanations is the tall-grass, or true, prairie. When people speak of the prairie, technically this is the area to which they are referring. The word is from the French word for meadow, because the area was discovered by the French explorers Marquette and Joliet in 1673. The tall-grass prairie has some of the most fertile soils on the earth and is now, roughly, the Corn Belt.

The native grasses in the tall-grass prairie grow taller than a person and the soil is black from the accumulation of centuries worth of rotted grass roots. The climate is more humid than that of the short- or mixed-grass prairie and toward the eastern end the soil is moist all the way to the water table. The tall-grass prairie also has its counterparts in other areas of the world — the pampas of Argentina and the Black Earth Belt of Russia. Some of the dominant grasses of the American tall-grass prairie are Big Bluestem (*Andropogon gerardi*), Indian Grass (*Sorghastrum nutans*), and Switch Grass (*Panicum virgatum*).

In general, the climate seems to be humid enough to support tree growth, but there is still debate about whether trees ever grew there, and if not, why not. People often note that trees planted in the prairie do well, but this is a meaningless observation because planted trees have been protected in the seedling stage — a precarious period for a plant in the wild — and they are protected from competition by having the grass around them cut. Present-day prairie reserves face constant invasion by trees and shrubs. But some people claim that trees could never invade the prairie.

Measurements in adjoining tracts of prairie and forest, where the weather and the soils are the same, show that each area tends to create conditions that lead to its own perpetuation. For instance, it is windier and hotter near ground level on the prairie than in the forest because there is nothing to break the wind or shade the soil. Consequently, there is more evaporation and less soil moisture in the prairie. These conditions favor plants that are adapted to dry conditions, i.e., grasses. In the forest area it is shady and the soil is damper — conditions that favor the growth of trees. As was pointed out before, once a dense prairie sod is established, it is hard for other seedlings to compete. So it appears that perhaps a vicious-circle effect is operating that might contribute to the maintenance of the prairie.

One theory about the origin of the prairies is that they developed after the retreat of the Wisconsin glacier, some 18,000 years ago. The climate then was apparently much drier than it is now. Fossil records from various parts of the Midwest indicate that grasses were there after the glacier but not before, and they seem to have remained there since. Once the prairie became established, it is believed by many that it was maintained by the grazing of the buffalo and by Indian fires.

Early prairie travelers wrote of the fires that "obscure the sun, moon, and stars for many days, or until the winter rains descend to quench the fire and purge the thick, ropey air, which is seen, tasted, handled, and felt." A more positively disposed traveler in 1824 called a prairie fire a "sublime spectacle," more spectacular than "the old Atlantic in his fury, a thunderstorm in the Alps, and the cataracts of Niagara." One man described a prairie fire thus:

> . . . a great number of hunters dispose themselves around a large prairie where herds of buffalo happen to be feeding, and setting fire to the grass, encompass them on all sides. The buffalo, having great fear of fire, retire toward the center of the prairie as they see it approach . . . and the Indians . . . slaughter immense numbers in a short period.

Many people believe that without these fires, the prairie would have been taken over by forest.

We have no way of knowing, because the tall-grass prairie no longer exists. It is now covered with corn, soybeans, houses, and factories. The plants of the tall-grass prairie — Big Bluestem, Indian Grass — can still be found in little relict patches such as the rights-of-way along railroad tracks. Also, throughout the tall-grass prairie region are reserves maintained by state governments or by private conservation organizations. The only significant area of unbroken prairie remaining is the Flint Hills region of eastern Kansas — four million acres that were too rocky to plow; this is one percent of the original tall-grass prairie. Conservation groups are presently trying to get parts of the Flint Hills made a national park.

Use and Abuse of Grasslands

When the European settlers came to New England they brought cattle with them and cattle needed food. Although New England is naturally forested, the river valleys and salt marshes provide extensive natural grasslands, and settlements started around these grasslands. The settlers were disappointed, however, with the quality of the grasses in the meadows — mainly Bluejoint (*Calamagrostis canadensis*) and Fowl Meadow Grass (*Poa palustris*). "Our beasts grow lousy with feeding upon it and are much out of heart and liking," wrote one man. So they soon started planting European forage grasses. Native prairie species, such as Big and Little Bluestem (*Andropogon* spp.), which are good forage species, do grow in New England, but not in wet places. If the colonists had discovered these, they perhaps would not have had to import grasses, but the Bluestems probably did not grow extensively in an essentially forested landscape.

The imported grasses did well here and quickly spread on their own. Many species were not only brought over deliberately but traveled here as seeds in the hay and manure on the ships. When the colonists arrived, they cleaned out the ships, the seeds germinated, and the plants spread. Some of our most common roadside species — Orchard Grass, Timothy, and others — were brought over here by the Europeans.

The Europeans' first exposure to prairies was in Ohio and Illinois, where the oak forest had many small prairie openings. This area could perhaps technically be termed a savanna, like the savannas of Africa — a grassy area with trees interspersed. Its origin is not really clear. Just as the tall-grass prairie boundary fluctuates to the west with that of the mixed-grass prairie, so it fluctuates to the east with that of the forest. Ohio and Indiana were perhaps all prairie in the dry period after the glaciers and perhaps the interspersal of grass and woods represents the gradual and uneven take-over of the prairie by the forest.

When confronted with the unbroken prairie — land that was to become the richest on earth — settlers' reactions were mixed. Europe is naturally forested, eastern North America is forested, and the settlers really did not understand grasslands. A few had the same reaction that many transcontinental travelers have today. One visitor to Chicago described Lake Michigan as "a waste . . . the fatiguing monotony of which is increased by the equally undiversified prospect of the land scenery, which affords no relief to the sight, as it consists merely of a plain, in which but a few patches of thin and scrubby woods are observed scattered here and there."

For a while there persisted the belief that since the prairie grew no trees it must have poor soil. However, most travelers saw it for what it was, and rejoiced in the openness and the richness of the land.

A Scottish farmer wrote in 1833:

The works of man are mere distortions compared with those of nature . . . The wide expanse appeared the gift of God to man for the exercise of his industry; and there being no obstacle to immediate cultivation, nature seemed inviting the husbandman to till the soil, and partake of her bounty. Mr. Malthus's doctrine, that population increases faster than the means of subsistence, appeared more than doubtful, and involving the unhallowed thought of a Being of infinite goodness and power leaving man, a favoured object of creation, without the means of subsistence. If a considerable portion of mankind ever are in want of food, the cause will be found to arise from human agency, and not from nature refusing to do her part. I felt grateful at beholding a field so well fitted to relieve the depressed and starving population of Great Britain and Ireland, while the conduct of their land-owning and tithe-eating legislators, in restricting the circulation of nature's bounty, appeared sinful.

Many were struck by the vastness of the area. A woman wrote, "When I saw a settler's child tripping out of home-bounds, I had a feeling that it would never get back again. It looked like putting out to Lake Michigan in a canoe." A man wrote, in 1824, "I do not know of anything that struck me more forcibly than the sensation of solitude I experienced in crossing this, and some of the other large Prairies. I was perfectly alone, and could see nothing in any direction but sky and grass . . . Not a living thing could I see or hear, except the occasional rising of some prairie fowl, or perhaps a large hawk or eagle wheeling about over my head. In the woods I have often experienced this silence and solitude, but it struck me more forcibly in these boundless meadows."

In spite of the fact that people realized the fertility of the soil, there were still many obstacles to prairie settlement. First, the prairie sod was so tough that plows used in the East were inadequate. Larger and heavier plows had to be invented, which required more oxen to pull. The biggest obstacle to prairie settlement was the lack of wood — for buildings, fuel, and fencing. A major breakthrough came with the invention of barbed wire in 1874.

West of the prairie, the Great Plains, or short-grass prairie, were similarly misunderstood. For pretty much the first half of the 1800s the Great Plains were assumed to be a desert. However, as soon as settlers began spending time there, either on their way to California in 1849 or during the construction of the railroad, they quickly learned that even if this land was unfit for agriculture, it was excellent for grazing. The cattle industry reached boom proportions in 1880, financed largely by European capital. Just as the Scottish farmer thought that the prairie would feed people forever, so the ranchers thought that the Great Plains would feed cattle forever, and they pushed the land beyond its capacity.

Cows will not eat everything green. They avoid some plants because they are poisonous, thorny, woody, or do not taste good. If there are not too many animals on a range, the grasses that they eat will grow back because grasses are adapted for doing this. However, if there are too many animals, they will graze the grasses too far, leaving them without enough photosynthetic tissue to survive. Furthermore, the constant trampling of animal hooves compacts the soil and makes it harder for water to infiltrate, so that it is drier below the surface. As the palatable species die out, the unpalatable species become more abundant, since they no longer have to compete with the native perennial grasses. Eventually, the whole range is covered with unpalatable species — sagebrush, mesquite, cactus, to name a few. If this process is stopped early enough, the grass will come back. However, if undesirable species become firmly established, the grass will never come back. The only way to bring it back is to plow the land under and reseed it. This is not a description of a hypothetical situation but of a real one that has happened over countless acres of the country. It is estimated that through overuse the grazing capacity of the Great Plains has been reduced to half of what it used to be.

Our grasslands are still vitally important to our economy in many ways. However, two ways in which they are used are symptomatic of the waste in our economy and of our luxurious lifestyle: the beef and lawn industries.

First, a word on cows. Cows are equipped to do something we cannot do, which is to digest cellulose. They can eat grass leaves and turn them into protein, whereas we can only digest the grain. The keeping of livestock was a brilliant development, for it meant that otherwise unusable land — land too dry to grow crops — could still produce human food.

Most of the remaining short-grass prairie of the United States is used for grazing calves. After a certain age the calves are sent to feed lots, where they spend the rest of their lives before they are slaughtered for beef. Most of the tall-grass prairie is planted with corn and soybeans, which are fed to the cattle in the feed lots. This grassland, however, could be used for something else — we could eat the corn and soybeans ourselves.* A diet of combined grasses and legumes can provide the necessary protein for human nutrition. To raise protein in a vegetable form and then feed it to an animal results not in more but less protein for us, for the animal is an inefficient converter. A rough figure for the conversion of vegetable protein to animal protein by all livestock is 8:1. For cattle, the ratio is closer to 21:1. The twenty pounds of vegetable protein that do not become meat become mainly manure, which is not used to fertilize fields, but is washed down the river.

Drive down a commercial strip outside any American city and it will not take long to figure out that Americans are fond of beef. Per capita consumption in this country is 129 lbs. per year, the highest in the world. The world economic system is such that if we stopped eating beef and ate grains and soybeans instead, the poorer countries of the world would unfortunately still not have any more to eat. However, it should be realized that a beef-oriented diet is inefficient and wasteful.

Grass is important in today's economy as forage for livestock, but it also forms the basis for another multimillion dollar business — the lawn industry. Sales of lawn seed, fertilizers, chemicals, and lawn paraphernalia are in the billions of dollars annually. We cannot eat lawns. They are not useful. To some, they are perhaps pleasant; to many they are an aggravation and a focus for feelings of social insecurity. Lawns do not maintain themselves. If you live in the eastern deciduous forest region,

* Soybeans are not a grass but a member of the Pea family, Leguminosae.

your lawn will do all it can to become a forest and will only stay lawn if energy — in the form of sweat, gas, and so forth — is expended. If you live in the desert, your lawn will try to revert to desert and will only stay a lawn if you water it. The desert does not naturally provide enough water to keep lawns green so this water must be mined from limited underground reserves or stolen from somewhere else. At least one million tons of fertilizer — manufactured with large quantities of natural gas — is used annually on lawns. If people like and can afford lawns, they should not be denied the pleasure of having them, but it should be realized again that to maintain a lawn to suburban standards is a luxury, not a necessity.

How to Use This Book

Identification in this book is based on drawings and descriptive notes of the plant's distinctive features. The plants are organized by visual similarity, not always by taxonomic grouping. An identification guide starts on p. 21. In using the pictures, remember that there is a tremendous amount of variation within each species, and the picture might not always look just like the plant you have found. In this case, make your decision on the basis of the written descriptions rather than the illustration. Remember that this book only describes common species and you might find a plant that is not in it. In that case, see p. 219.

Most plants have two names — a common name and a scientific name. The common names have developed informally over the centuries and vary from place to place and person to person. The scientific names — always in Latin — are given to the plant according to a more or less internationally accepted standardized system. The Latin name consists of two parts. The first, always capitalized, is the genus name — for instance, *Hordeum* (Barley). The second, usually in small letters, such as *vulgare* (common), is the species name. The full name of the species is *Hordeum vulgare*, or Common Barley. If we refer to *Hordeum vulgare* again in another sentence, or if we refer to another species of *Hordeum*, such as *Hordeum pusillum* (Little

Barley), we can abbreviate it to *H. vulgare* or *H. pusillum*. If you go to China and mention *Hordeum vulgare* to Chinese botanists, they will understand you. If you mention Barley, they may or may not. If you mention Rye, they might think you mean *Secale cereale* (cultivated Rye), or *Lolium perenne* (a lawn grass), or one of several species of the genus *Elymus*, commonly called Wild Rye.

The point of all this is that common names are not very reliable, and I have found them especially useless for grasses. The confusion that people often feel in dealing with grasses and grasslike plants reflects itself in their common names. Wiregrass, for instance, is a common name for the following species: *Andropogon scoparius*, *Aristida oligantha*, *Eleusine indica*, *Cynodon dactylon*, *Poa compressa*, and *Juncus tenuis*. These species have very few similarities, and *Juncus tenuis* is not even a grass, but a member of the Rush family. Spike Rush, or *Eleocharis*, is not a rush but a sedge. Black Grass, *Juncus gerardi*, is not a grass but a rush. Cotton Grass, *Eriophorum*, is not a grass but a sedge. So, aside from being vague, the common names for these plants are often inaccurate. Furthermore, many of them have no common names. For all of these reasons I have tried to avoid the use of common names in the text.

Although a scientific name might be the same all over the world, it unfortunately does not necessarily stay the same over time. Plants are often named incorrectly, and when the mistake is discovered, the name must be changed. Or a botanist might decide that the designation of species status to a certain group of plants is wrong and a name must either be discarded or invented. Some of the scientific names in this book are out-of-date for these reasons. However, for the sake of consistency and the convenience of the lay person who might refer to it, I have followed the nomenclature of *Gray's Manual of Botany*, 8th Edition. The common names I have taken from various sources.

Most of the plants described in this book grow throughout the northeastern United States, which is the area that the book covers. I have only noted ranges when they are restricted within the Northeast. For more detailed range information, consult *Gray's Manual*.

This book gives both metric and U.S. measurements, using the following set of equivalents: 25 millimeters or 2.5 centimeters per inch; 30 centimeters or 0.3 meter per foot. Plants vary considerably in height and the measurements are for convenience sake, in some cases, approximate.

Identification Guide

GLOSSARY FOR IDENTIFICATION GUIDE

inflorescence — the arrangement of the flowers on the stem; the entire assemblage of flowers.

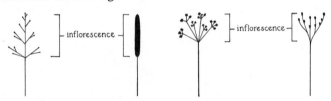

flower cluster — a small group of flowers, usually at the end of a stalk (technically known as a spikelet), made up of the **flower scales** (technically known as glumes, lemmas, and paleas). In the grasses and sedges, the flowers are small and have no showy petals, only stamens (male, pollen-bearing) and pistils (female, fruit-producing). The stamens and pistils are enclosed by the flower scales.

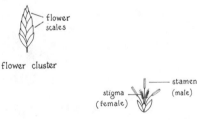

bract — a leaflike or bristly structure under the inflorescence.

Identification Guide

If your plant has a triangular stem, go to p. 24.

If your plant has a round stem with no branches in the inflorescence, go to p. 25. (Look closely and make sure it doesn't just have branches that are close together.)

If your plant has a round stem with flower branches forking from one point at the top, go to p. 26.

If your plant has a round stem with flowers coming out of one point on the side of the stem, go to pp. 122–123.

If your plant has a round stem with flower branches arranged vertically along the stem, go to p. 27.

Plants with a Triangular Stem

Flowers come out of the side of the stem
   Scirpus americanus p. 33
   Scirpus robustus p. 34

Branches radiate from one point at the top of the stem

1. Flowers are in flattened clusters in a featherlike arrangement.
   Cyperus pp. 40–44

2. Flowers are in three-dimensional clusters, round or egg-shaped.

side branches on the stem, but not much branching in the inflorescence; no long leafy bracts under the inflorescence	no side branches on the stem, but much branching in the inflorescence; long leafy bracts under the inflorescence
Cladium p. 45	*Scirpus* pp. 33–39
Rhynchospora p. 46	

Flowers or flower clusters are lined vertically along the stem
  Carex pp. 47–62

PLANTS WITH A ROUND STEM AND NO BRANCHES
IN THE INFLORESCENCE

Inflorescence is conical
  Eleocharis ⎤
  Equisetum ⎬ pp. 63–66
  Allium ⎦
  Bulbostylis p. 121

Inflorescence is cylindrical; bristly in silhouette
  Hordeum ⎤   *Aristida* pp. 96–98
  Setaria   *Tripsacum* p. 104
  Triticum
  Secale
  Elymus ⎬ pp. 67–83
  Hystrix
  Anthoxanthum
  Koeleria
  Distichlis ⎦

Inflorescence is cylindrical but not bristly in silhouette
  Triticum p. 72   *Tripsacum* p. 104
  Phleum ⎤   *Spartina* pp. 124–129
  Ammophila   *Sporobolus* p. 186
  Alopecurus
  Typha ⎬ pp. 84–92
  Acorus
  Plantago ⎦

Inflorescence is flat
> *Agropyron*⎤
> *Lolium* ⎬ pp. 93–95
> *Paspalum*⎦

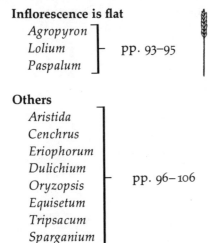

Others
> *Aristida*⎤
> *Cenchrus*⎟
> *Eriophorum*⎟
> *Dulichium*⎟
> *Oryzopsis* ⎬ pp. 96–106
> *Equisetum*⎟
> *Tripsacum*⎟
> *Sparganium*⎦
> *Andropogon* p. 132

Plants with a Round Stem and Flower Branches Forking from one Point at the Top of the Stem

Flowers are lined continuously along the branches with no space between them
> *Paspalum* p. 95
> *Digitaria*⎤
> *Cynodon* ⎟
> *Eleusine* ⎬ pp. 107–111
> *Andropogon*⎦

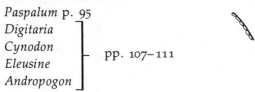

Flowers are lined along the branches with space between them
> *Juncus* pp. 112–119; 122

Flowers are in clusters at the end of the branches
> *Scirpus cyperinus* p. 36
> *Cladium* p. 45

Rhynchospora p. 46
Juncus
Luzula   ⎱ pp. 112–122
Bulbostylis ⎰

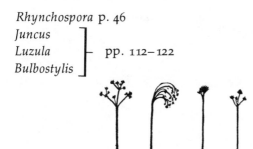

Plants with a Round Stem and Flower Branches Arranged Vertically

Seeds are lined tightly along one side of each branch
Paspalum p. 95
Spartina pp. 124–129

Branches are all along the stem, starting near the bottom, mixed in with the leaves; seeds are fuzzy
Andropogon pp. 130–132

Plants are big (more than 6 ft.); inflorescence is fuzzy and plumelike
Phragmites ⎱ pp. 134–137
Miscanthus ⎰

All the branches droop
1. Inflorescence is narrow; branches are short
   Muhlenbergia p. 133
   Brachyelytrum p. 138
   Bouteloua p. 139

2. Inflorescence is delicate; branches are thin and wiry, and the flowers overlap very little

Glyceria
Triodia
Hierochloë pp. 140–147   *Agrostis* pp. 152–157
Leersia
Deschampsia

3. Inflorescence is relatively coarse, with much overlapping of flowers and branches.

   a. flower scales have little bristles on the end
      Bromus pp. 148–151
      Festuca pp. 170–173

   b. flower scales have no bristles
      Phragmites p. 134   *Poa* pp. 191–196
      Hierochloë p. 144   *Festuca* p. 197
      Echinochloa pp. 183–185   *Calamagrostis* p. 201
      Glyceria p. 187

The branches do not droop, or only a few of them do.
This is the hardest group and the reason that people often think all grasses look alike. Within this group are several subcategories:

1. Inflorescence is roundish, bunchy.
   Andropogon pp. 130–132
   Dactylis p. 174

2. Inflorescence is sparse and delicate, not full; branches are thin and wiry, naked for much of their length.

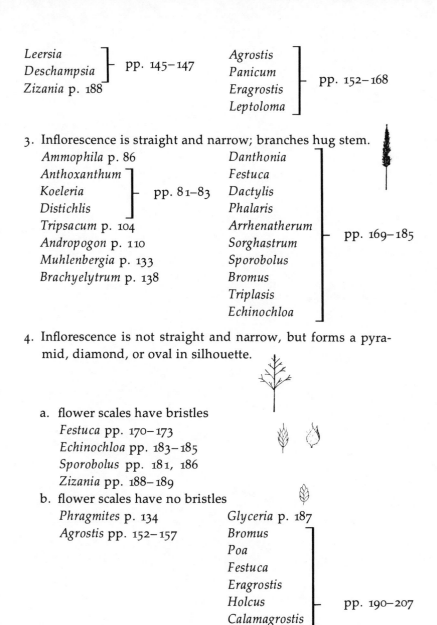

Leersia	
Deschampsia	pp. 145–147
Zizania p. 188	

Agrostis	
Panicum	
Eragrostis	pp. 152–168
Leptoloma	

3. Inflorescence is straight and narrow; branches hug stem.

Ammophila p. 86		Danthonia	
Anthoxanthum		Festuca	
Koeleria	pp. 81–83	Dactylis	
Distichlis		Phalaris	
Tripsacum p. 104		Arrhenatherum	
Andropogon p. 110		Sorghastrum	pp. 169–185
Muhlenbergia p. 133		Sporobolus	
Brachyelytrum p. 138		Bromus	
		Triplasis	
		Echinochloa	

4. Inflorescence is not straight and narrow, but forms a pyramid, diamond, or oval in silhouette.

a. flower scales have bristles
   Festuca pp. 170–173
   Echinochloa pp. 183–185
   Sporobolus pp. 181, 186
   Zizania pp. 188–189
b. flower scales have no bristles
   Phragmites p. 134
   Agrostis pp. 152–157

Glyceria p. 187	
Bromus	
Poa	
Festuca	
Eragrostis	
Holcus	pp. 190–207
Calamagrostis	
Cinna	
Avena	
Zea	

*Species Descriptions
and Illustrations*

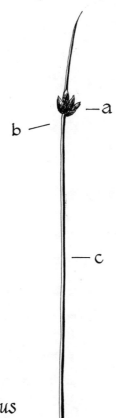

b —

— a

— c

Three ~ square
Scirpus americanus

Sword Grass, Chairmaker's Rush
Sedge family   Cyperaceae

a scaly brown flower clusters come out of the side of the stem, with no stalks
b no leafy bracts under inflorescence
c triangular stem

great variation in height: 3 cm–1.5 m (1¼ in.–5 ft.)

freshwater, brackish, or salt marshes
native
perennial

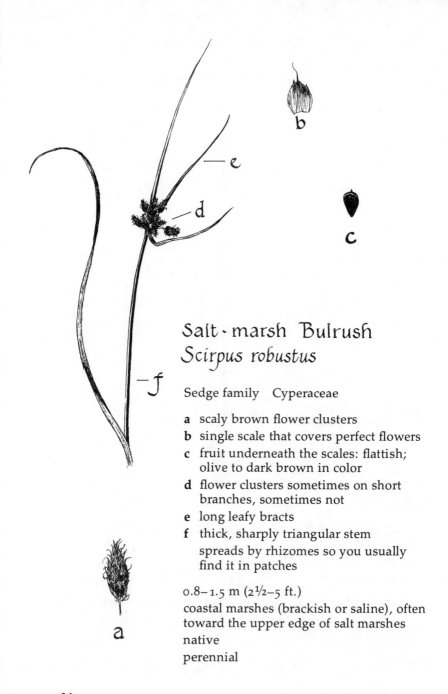

Salt‑marsh Bulrush
Scirpus robustus

Sedge family   Cyperaceae

a scaly brown flower clusters
b single scale that covers perfect flowers
c fruit underneath the scales: flattish; olive to dark brown in color
d flower clusters sometimes on short branches, sometimes not
e long leafy bracts
f thick, sharply triangular stem spreads by rhizomes so you usually find it in patches

0.8–1.5 m (2½–5 ft.)
coastal marshes (brackish or saline), often toward the upper edge of salt marshes
native
perennial

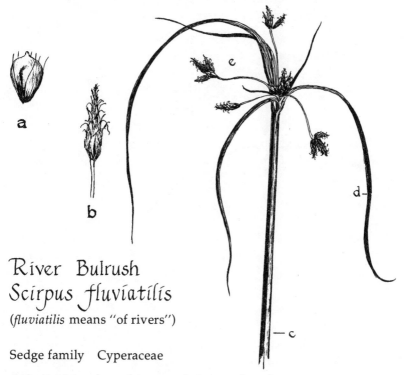

River Bulrush
Scirpus fluviatilis

(*fluviatilis* means "of rivers")

Sedge family   Cyperaceae

a fruit triangular; white to pale brown in color
b scaly brown flower clusters
c thick triangular stem
d long leafy bracts
e widely branching inflorescence often with several flower clusters at the end of each branch

68 cm–2 m (27 in.–7 ft.)
freshwater marshes, lake and stream borders; often in large colonies
native
perennial

This species and *S. robustus* could be confused, but *S. fluviatilis* grows in fresh water, *S. robustus* in salt and brackish water. *S. fluviatilis* has a more widely branching inflorescence. The fruit of *S. fluviatilis* is a pale color; that of *S. robustus* dark green to black.

a

— b

— d

— c Wool Grass
Scirpus cyperinus

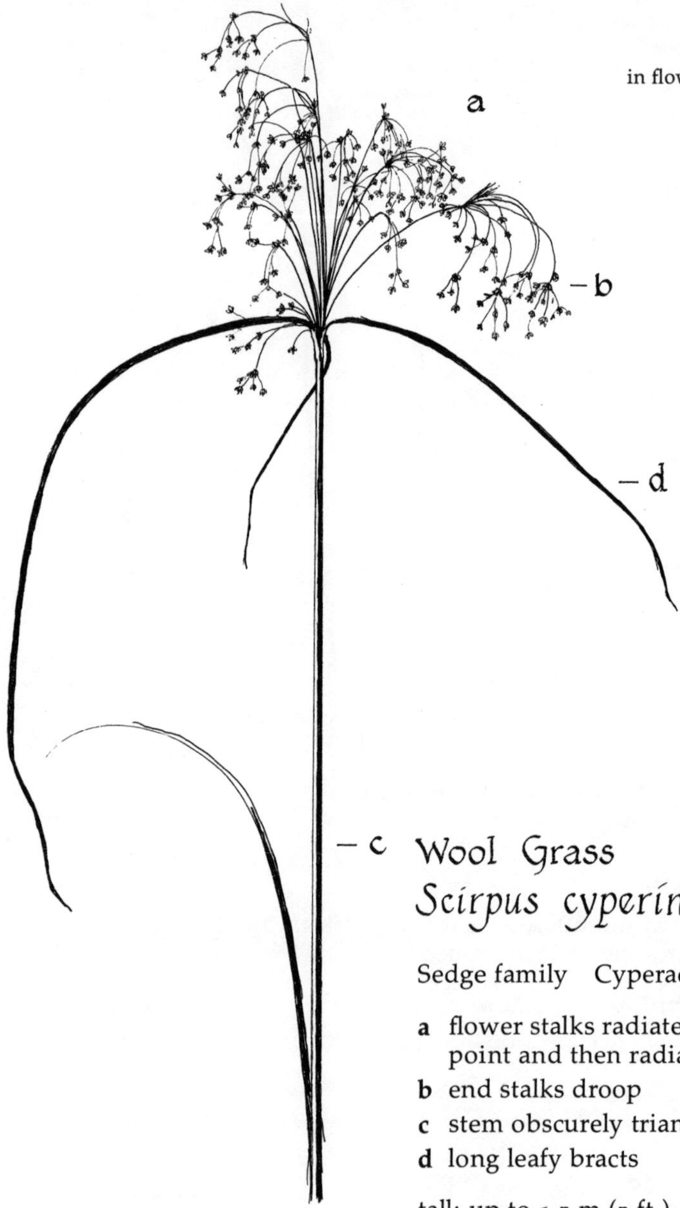

Sedge family   Cyperaceae

a flower stalks radiate out from one
point and then radiate again
b end stalks droop
c stem obscurely triangular
d long leafy bracts

tall: up to 1.5 m (5 ft.)
grows in clumps in wet places
native
perennial

in fruit (late summer–fall);
    very fuzzy, brown

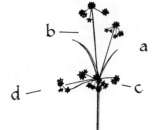

Dark Green Bulrush
Scirpus atrovirens

Sedge family   Cyperaceae

a relatively few branches
      in the inflorescence
b often the vertical
      branches are longer than the others
c branches radiate from the top of the stem,
      then usually branch no more than once
      again
d flowers in round clusters, various shades
      of brown
e triangular stem

medium-size to tall: 30 cm–1.8 m (1–6 ft.)
wet places
native
perennial
appears late in spring, disintegrates by late summer

S. atrovirens and *S. rubrotinctus* could be confused.
S. atrovirens has bigger and fewer flower clusters and they are
brown, not green. *S. atrovirens* has no red on the stem.
S. atrovirens could possibly be confused with *Juncus canadensis*
(p. 116) which has a round stem and round leaves.
The flower clusters of *Scirpus* disintegrate if you rub them
between your fingers; those of *Juncus* do not.

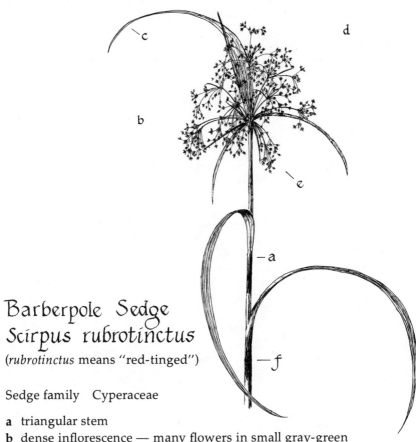

Barberpole Sedge
Scirpus rubrotinctus
(*rubrotinctus* means "red-tinged")

Sedge family   Cyperaceae

a triangular stem
b dense inflorescence — many flowers in small gray-green
clusters
c leafy bracts
d inflorescence almost circular in outline
e branches radiate from one point at the top of the stem, then
radiate again and again
f bands of dark red on the leaf sheath

medium-size: less than 1 m (3½ ft.)
more common northward; abundant in wet meadows in
northern New England
native
perennial
appears in late spring; disintegrates by late summer

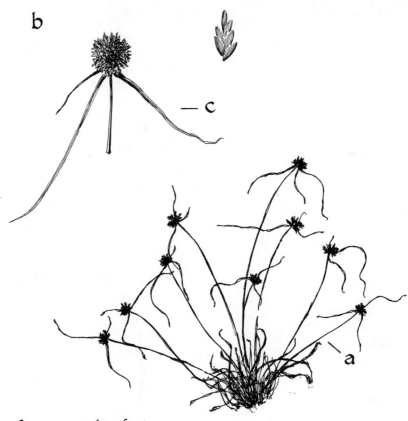

Cyperus filiculmis
(*fili* means "thread" and *culm* means "stem")

Sedge family   Cyperaceae

a wiry triangular stem
b round inflorescences, sometimes with branches
c shriveled curly bracts
    gray-green

small: 5–90 cm (2 in.–3 ft.)
usually grows in tufts in sandy soil
native
perennial

Umbrella Sedge
Cyperus strigosus

Galingale
Sedge family   Cyperaceae

a branches radiate from the top of the stem
b flower scales yellow-green
c flat flower clusters arranged perpendicular to branch, like a bottle brush
d leafy bracts
e triangular stem

medium-size, up to 1 m (3½ ft.) but usually around 30 cm (1 ft.)
moist ground, shores and meadows; commonly as a weed in moist bare soil
native
perennial

This species and *Cyperus esculentus* (next) are similar. *C. esculentus* has little hard tubers at the end of the stolons, but if you don't have the underground part of the plant to look at, you must decide on the basis of the size of the flower scales. On *C. strigosus* they are 4 mm (⅙ in.) long or longer; on *C. esculentus* they are 4 mm or less. This is not always an easy distinction to make. The flower clusters of *C. strigosus* tend to be denser, but this is not a reliable characteristic.

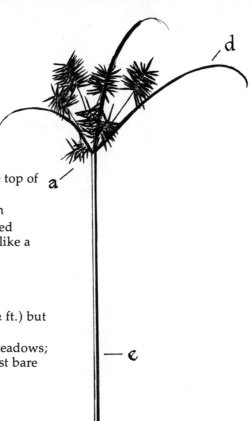

Nut Sedge
Cyperus esculentus
(*esculentus* means "edible")

Yellow Nut-grass
Sedge family   Cyperaceae

a flower branches radiate from the top of the stem
b flower scales yellow-green
c flat flower clusters perpendicular to branch, like a bottle brush
d leafy bracts
e triangular stem
f hard little tubers underground

20–90 cm (8 in.–3 ft.)
damp, sandy soil; can be troublesome weed
native
perennial

An African variety of this species, *C. esculentus* var. *sativus*, rarely flowers and instead has many crowded tubers. It is known as Chufa, and is planted in the southeastern U.S. for its edible tubers.

a

d

e

c

b

f

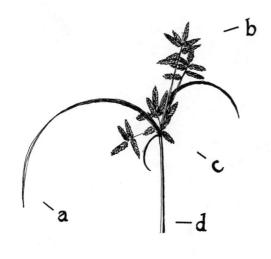

Cyperus diandrus
Cyperus rivularis

Sedge family   Cyperaceae

a   three leafy bracts
b   flower clusters arranged horizontally or pointing slightly downward from the stalk
c   branches radiate from one point at the top of the stem
d   triangular stem
e   flower scales in a flattened cluster, each scale tinged with red, or sometimes all red

small: 2.5–45 cm (1–18 in.)
grows in tufts in damp places, often on shores
native
annual
midsummer–fall

These two species are very similar and often grow inter-mingled with each other. The differences between them are hard to see without a magnifying glass.

44

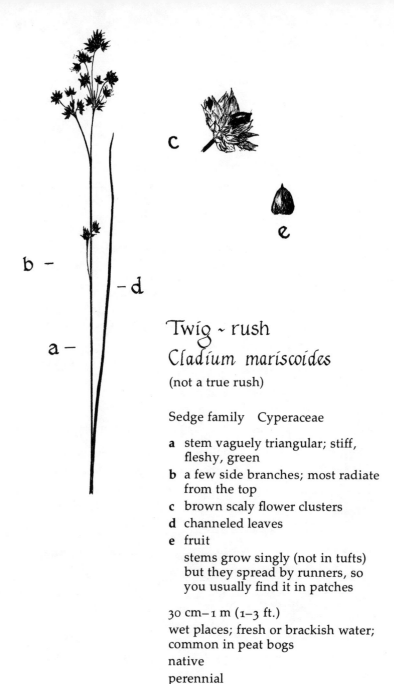

c

e

b –

a –

– d

Twig – rush
Cladium mariscoides
(not a true rush)

Sedge family   Cyperaceae

a stem vaguely triangular; stiff,
   fleshy, green
b a few side branches; most radiate
   from the top
c brown scaly flower clusters
d channeled leaves
e fruit
   stems grow singly (not in tufts)
   but they spread by runners, so
   you usually find it in patches

30 cm–1 m (1–3 ft.)
wet places; fresh or brackish water;
common in peat bogs
native
perennial

45

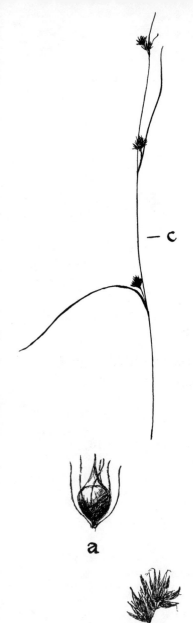

Beak ~ rush
Rhynchospora spp.
(not a true rush)

Sedge family   Cyperaceae

a distinctive fruit
b irregularly shaped scaly brown
flower clusters
c thin weak green stems, vaguely
triangular

can grow up to 1.5 m (5 ft.) but is
usually smaller
wet places
native
mainly perennial; summer flowering

This genus contains many similar
species, distinguished from each
other mainly by characteristics of
the fruit — texture, color, length of
bristles, and so forth.
   Cladium (preceding) and
Rhynchospora are easily confused.
In general, *Cladium* has stiffer, fatter
stems. The surest difference,
however, is in the fruits.
Rhynchospora fruits always have a
protuberance on the top, called the
beak or *tubercle,* which *Cladium*
fruits do not have.

The genus Carex

The genus *Carex*, or Sedge, is a huge worldwide genus. *Gray's Manual of Botany* describes 267 species, making it the largest genus in eastern North America. Unfortunately for the lay person, many of these species look very similar. Fortunately, many of them are relatively uncommon and not often seen. In our range, all of the species are perennial and almost all of them are native. Most grow in wet places or in woods. In the United States, the genus has little economic importance and sedges have not been valued as forage. A few species of *Carex* can be found in the prairie, but they do not dominate. In other parts of the world, however, particularly mountainous, arctic and subarctic areas, various species of *Carex* are used as forage and are even cultivated. Sedges are also sometimes used as fiber for making mats and other objects.

The genus as a whole is easy to recognize. The flowers are unisexual — that is, the male and female parts are borne on separate flowers. Sometimes the two sexes are borne on separate inflorescences, sometimes together. The distinguishing feature of the genus is that each female flower is enclosed in a sac called the *perigynium* (*peri* means "around" and *gyn* refers to female reproductive parts). Sometimes this sac is inflated and easy to see, as in *C. lupulina* (p. 58) or *C. intumescens* (p. 59); sometimes it is thin and closely bound to the flower, as in *C. scoparia* (p. 52).

e —

d —

— c

Carex laxiflora

a

Sedge family   Cyperaceae

a grows in leafy tufts
b dead leaves from pre-
    vious years
c leafy bracts under each
    flower stalk

— b

d female inflorescence consists of small blunt-tipped sacs
e male inflorescence
    flower stalks might become longer as flowers ripen

20–60 cm (8 in.–2 ft.)
mostly in woods
native
perennial

This is one species of a large group within the genus *Carex*,
known as the *Laxiflorae*. The species in this group are quite
similar and are distinguished by technical characteristics.
They all flower in the spring and the flowering stalks wither
by midsummer after the fruit has ripened. However, you will
find the basal leaves throughout the year.

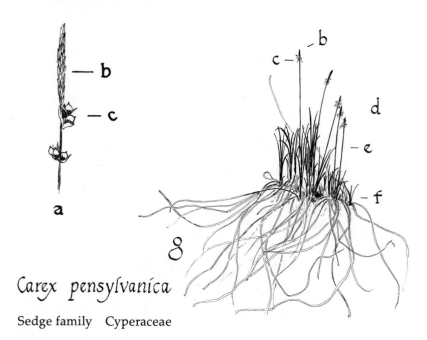

Carex pensylvanica

Sedge family   Cyperaceae

flowers very early in the spring, before the leaves are out on
the trees

a in fruit
b male flowers (club-shaped inflorescence)
c female flowers
d inflorescence brown to reddish purple
e triangular stems
f red, fibrous at base
g last year's dead leaves

small: less than 40 cm (16 in.)
native
perennial

This is a plant you could walk right past even though it is one
of the most common ground-layer species in dry oak woods.
If you try to pull up a tuft of it, you will end up pulling up a
patch because it spreads by stolons and thus manages to cover
large areas of ground. Although the flower stalks disintegrate
by late spring, the thin leaves remain throughout the year.

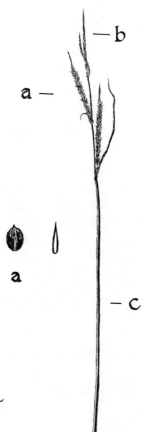

Tussock Sedge
Carex stricta

Sedge family   Cyperaceae

a female flower clusters are thin and narrow; reddish to purple brown; made up of small flat sacs
b male flower clusters (tan, shaggy)
c rough triangular stem
d tussocks, 60–90 cm (2–3 ft.) high

up to 1.4 m (4½ ft.), usually shorter
native
perennial

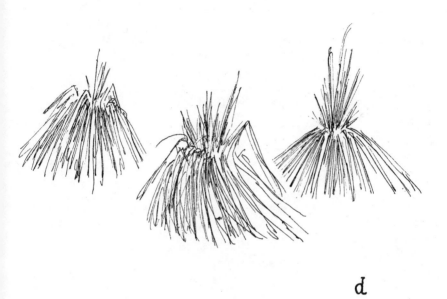

d

The plants form big tussocks in wet places. You have
probably tried to cross a little swamp by jumping from one
clump to the other and found out that they are not very stable.
The flowering stalks appear from May to August but
disintegrate fairly quickly, so the best way to recognize this
sedge is by the big leafy tussocks.

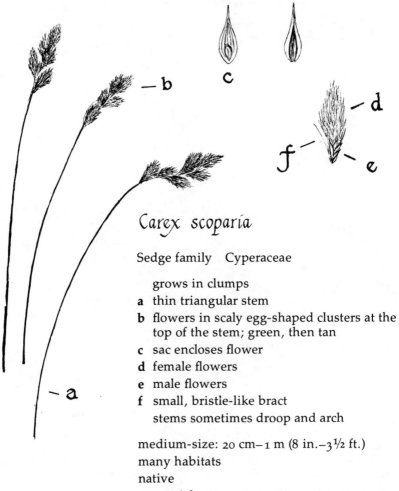

Carex scoparia

Sedge family   Cyperaceae

   grows in clumps
- **a** thin triangular stem
- **b** flowers in scaly egg-shaped clusters at the top of the stem; green, then tan
- **c** sac encloses flower
- **d** female flowers
- **e** male flowers
- **f** small, bristle-like bract
   stems sometimes droop and arch

medium-size: 20 cm–1 m (8 in.–3½ ft.)
many habitats
native
perennial

This is one species of a large group within the genus *Carex* called the *Ovales*. All of the species look much like this one and are very hard to tell apart. They have a variety of habitats, from swamps and woods to dry sand. *Carex scoparia* is one of the more common species.

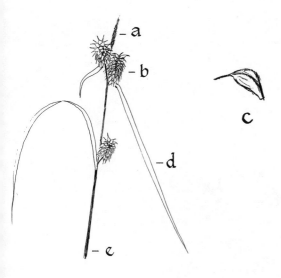

Carex flava
(*flava* means "yellow")

Sedge family Cyperaceae

  yellow-green
a male inflorescence
b female inflorescence
c small inflated sacs with beaks pointing downward
d long leafy bracts
e triangular stem

small: 10–75 cm (4 in.–2½ ft.)
grows in clumps in wet meadows
and shores, often in profusion
native
perennial

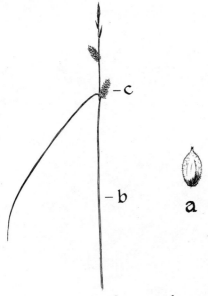

Carex lanuginosa

Sedge family   Cyperaceae

flowering shoots inconspicuous among the leaves; often grows in big patches
a small, slightly fuzzy flower sac with short toothed beak
b thin stems
c small flower clusters: 2.5–7.5 cm (1–3 in.)
spreads by rhizomes

up to 1 m (3½ ft.)
meadows, shores
native
perennial

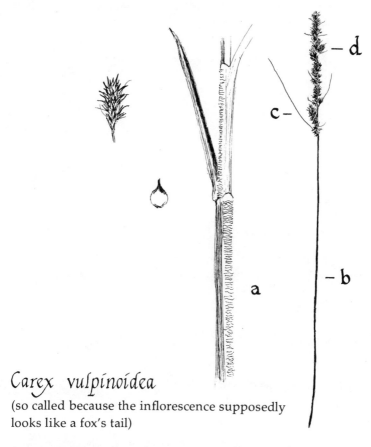

Carex vulpinoidea
(so called because the inflorescence supposedly
looks like a fox's tail)

Sedge family   Cyperaceae

a puckering at base of stem
b stiff triangular stem
c bristle-like bracts under and throughout inflorescence
d narrow asymmetrical inflorescence

medium-size: 20 cm–1 m (8 in.–3½ ft.)
grows in clumps in wet places
native
perennial
June–August

Carex stipata

Sedge family   Cyperaceae

yellow-green, then turns brown while stem stays green
a   irregularly shaped inflorescence with few short branches
b   spongy fat triangular stem
c   slightly inflated sac, widest and somewhat spongy at the base
d   two small teeth; long beak
e   puckering at base of stem

medium-size: 40–90 cm (16 in.–3 ft.)
grows in clumps in wet places
native
perennial
flowers mainly in the spring and disintegrates by late summer

C. stipata and *C. vulpinoidea* (preceding) could be confused but *C. stipata* is fatter and spongier, both in the stem and in the flower sacs, and its flower sacs are bigger. *C. vulpinoidea* usually has more visible thin bracts throughout the inflorescence.

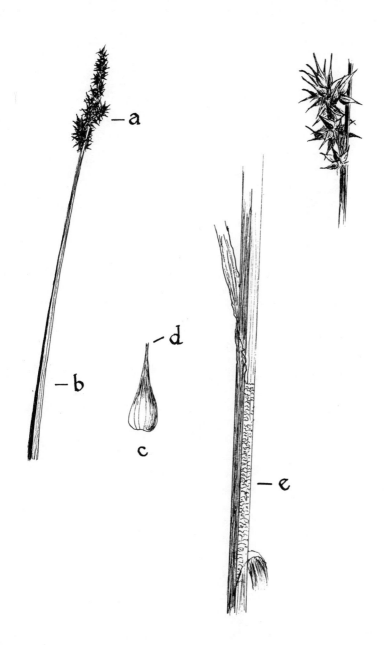

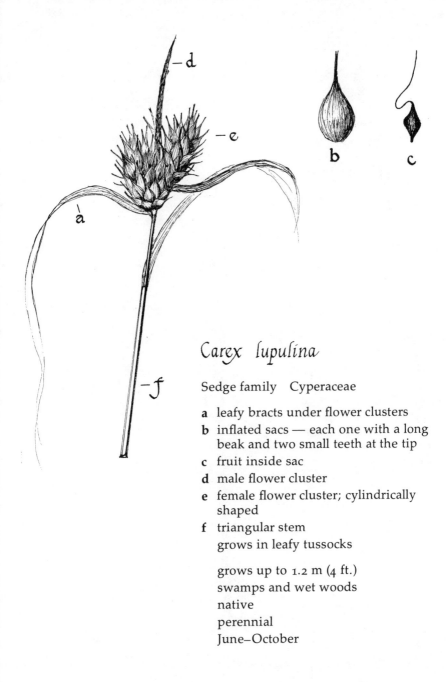

Carex lupulina

Sedge family   Cyperaceae

a leafy bracts under flower clusters
b inflated sacs — each one with a long
   beak and two small teeth at the tip
c fruit inside sac
d male flower cluster
e female flower cluster; cylindrically
   shaped
f triangular stem
   grows in leafy tussocks

grows up to 1.2 m (4 ft.)
swamps and wet woods
native
perennial
June–October

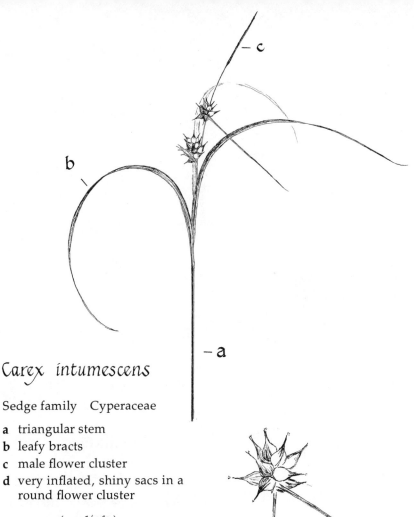

Carex intumescens

Sedge family   Cyperaceae

a triangular stem
b leafy bracts
c male flower cluster
d very inflated, shiny sacs in a
   round flower cluster

30–75 cm (1–2½ ft.)
grows in clumps in wet soil
native
perennial
late May–September

C. intumescens, C. lupulina, and *C. folliculata* could be
confused. Of the three, *C. intumescens* has the most inflated
sacs, then *C. lupulina,* then *C. folliculata.* The inflorescences of
C. intumescens are round in outline, not cylindrical. The
inflorescences of *C. folliculata* are far apart from each other.

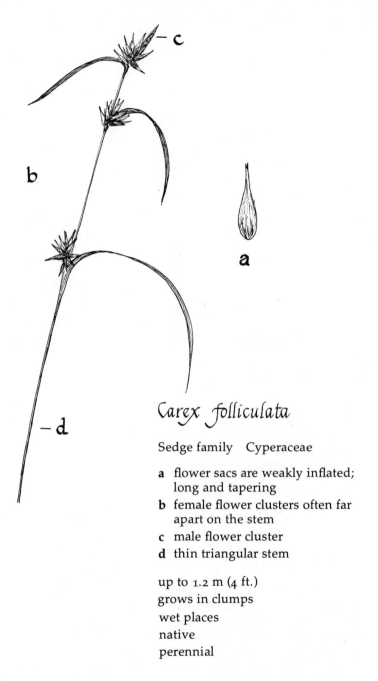

Carex folliculata

Sedge family   Cyperaceae

a flower sacs are weakly inflated; long and tapering
b female flower clusters often far apart on the stem
c male flower cluster
d thin triangular stem

up to 1.2 m (4 ft.)
grows in clumps
wet places
native
perennial

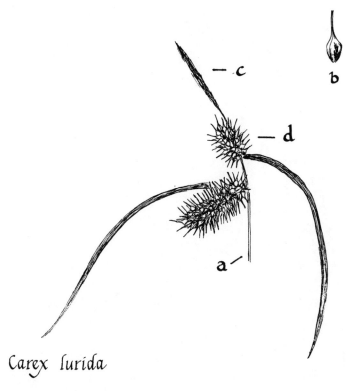

Carex lurida

Sedge family   Cyperaceae

a triangular stem
b flower sacs small; slightly inflated, with straight beak
c male flower cluster
d female flower cluster cylindrically shaped, with many flower sacs: 1.2–7.5 cm (½–3 in.)

varies in size: 20 cm–1 m (8 in–3½ ft.)
grows in clumps in wet soil
native
perennial

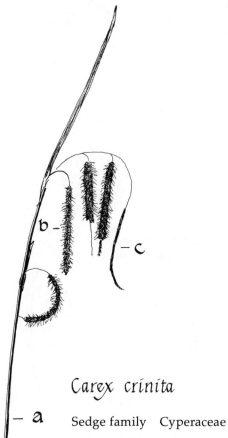

Carex crinita

Sedge family   Cyperaceae

a triangular stem
b drooping, bristly female
    inflorescence
c male inflorescence

30 cm–1.6 m (1–5½ ft.)
grows in clumps in wet places; very
common in northern areas
native
perennial

Spike Rush
Eleocharis acicularis

(*acicularis* means "needle-shaped")

Sedge family   Cyperaceae

> tiny plant: 2.5–30 cm (1 in.–1 ft.)
> very thin stems
> often forms large mats; hard to separate from the mud
> where it grows

damp shores
native
perennial

The genus *Eleocharis* has several species, all similar and all very variable. They have leafless stems and a single conical flower cluster at the top. They grow in wet places; in fact, the name comes from the Greek *elos*, for marsh. They are distinguished from each other mainly on the basis of the structure of the fruit, as well as certain details of the stem. *E. acicularis* and *E. obtusa* are two of the more common species; however, you could easily find others. The whole genus is referred to as Spike Rush although it is not in the Rush family.

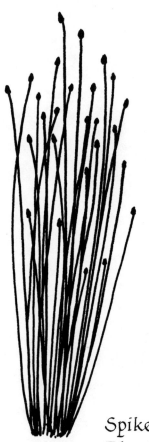

Spike Rush
Eleocharis obtusa

Sedge family   Cyperaceae

   conical inflorescence, one on each stem
   soft stems; sometimes fat, sometimes thin
   detail of fruit shown

grows in clumps to a height of 75 cm (2½ ft.)
native
perennial

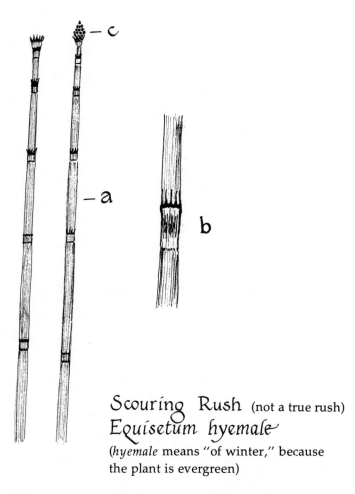

Scouring Rush (not a true rush)
Equisetum hyemale
(*hyemale* means "of winter," because
the plant is evergreen)

Horsetail family   Equisetaceae

a rough, hollow stem with no branches
b toothed black bands
c reproductive structure

up to 3 m (10 ft.)
wet places
native
perennial

a

Field Garlic
Allium vineale

Lily family   Liliaceae

a bulb at base
   onion smell

up to 1.2 m (4 ft.)
fields, roadsides
alien
perennial

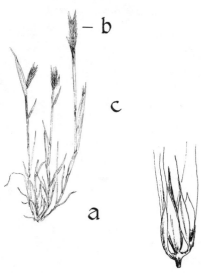

Little Barley
Hordeum pusillum
(*pusillum* means "very small")

Grass family   Gramineae

a grows in little tufts
b flower clusters in two distinct rows
c stiff straight inflorescence

small: less than 40 cm (16 in.)
fields, roadsides, dry sandy soil
rarely found in New England; more common in the Midwest
native
annual
May–June

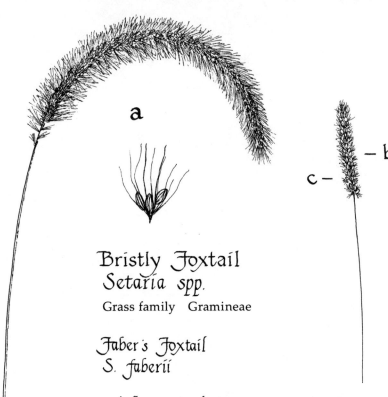

Bristly Foxtail
Setaria spp.
Grass family   Gramineae

Faber's Foxtail
S. faberii

a inflorescence droops

the biggest of the three: up to 1.8 m (6 ft.)
a recent introduction to this continent

Yellow Foxtail
S. glauca
Pigeon Grass

b stiff straight inflorescence
c yellow-brown hairs

10 cm–1.2 m (4 in.–4 ft.)

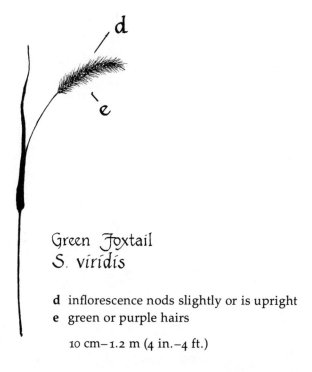

Green Foxtail
S. viridis

d inflorescence nods slightly or is upright
e green or purple hairs

10 cm–1.2 m (4 in.–4 ft.)

Species in the genus *Setaria* (Bristly Foxtail) have a flexible cylindrical inflorescence with many short fine hairs. If you squeeze the inflorescence through your hand, it will wiggle like a woolly bear caterpillar. A cultivated species in the genus is Millet, *S. italica,* grown for food in the Near East and China. In our area there are three common species, all weedy annuals. Being annuals, these plants produce many seeds and are a valuable food source for birds. The name *Setaria* comes from the Latin *seta,* for bristle.

Squirreltail Grass
Hordeum jubatum

Grass family   Gramineae

a early flowering stage: light green
b in flower: shining green to purple
c after fruit has ripened: bleached tan
      inflorescence falls apart easily once you pick it
d single flower cluster in ripe fruit

grows low to the ground: 30–75 cm (1–2½ ft.)
roadsides, fields, meadows, open soil
apparently native
annual, biennial, or perennial

Considered beautiful by botanists and a noxious weed by
ranchers because the bristles pierce animals' tongues and can
cause serious injury.

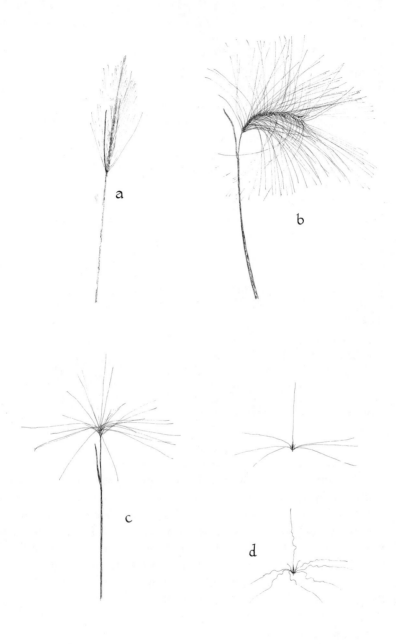

a

b

c

d

Wheat
Triticum aestivum

Grass family   Gramineae

a flower clusters are fat and round
sometimes has bristles, sometimes not
blue-green, then tan

60 cm–1 m (2–3½ ft.)
roadsides, fields
alien
annual

This is one of the three most important grain crops of the
world (the other two being Corn and Rice). Rice grows in the
tropics, Corn grows from the semi-tropics to temperate areas,
and Wheat grows where it is too cold or dry for Corn.
Although Wheat is adaptable to a wide variety of soil and
climatic conditions, it cannot tolerate a combination of high
heat and humidity. Wheat is the dominant cereal of Europe
and western Asia and has been the staple food of western
civilization for a long time. As with any agricultural crop,
there are countless varieties. Some, called winter wheats, can
be planted in the fall. The young plants withstand the winter,
and they are ready for harvest in July. Spring wheats are
planted in March for harvest in autumn.

   Wheat is distinguished by the presence of gluten, a
combination of proteins that makes dough stick together and
thus makes bread possible. Modern milling processes, which
produce white flour, remove the outer layers of the wheat
grain where most of the vitamins and minerals are found, and
the germ, or embryo, where most of the protein is contained.
This is fed to livestock and we are left with food of such poor
nutritional quality that the flour is then "enriched" with
synthetic vitamins and minerals.

a

Rye
Secale cereale

a   b

Grass family   Gramineae

a single flower, toothed fringe on edge of scales
b grain
c stiff bristles, all about the same length
d inflorescence is heavy; often droops when ripe
   green at first, yellow when ripe

60 cm–1 m (2–3½ ft.)
annual

This is the Rye of rye bread — a cultivated grain crop. As
such, you will often find it growing in fallow fields or along
roadsides in agricultural areas. It is also sometimes planted in
bare soil to control erosion.

   Rye can tolerate colder conditions than any other cereal, so it
is mainly cultivated in northern Europe and Russia. It is also
the most adaptable of the cereals to poor soil and is sometimes
called "poverty grain." In spite of its virtues, however, it
takes a definite second to Wheat in popularity for making
bread. Most of the Rye grown in the U.S. is grown for animal
feed.

   Could be confused with *Elymus canadensis* (p. 78) which has
curving bristles. *Elymus virginicus* (p. 79) does not droop;
flower clusters are shaped differently (as shown).

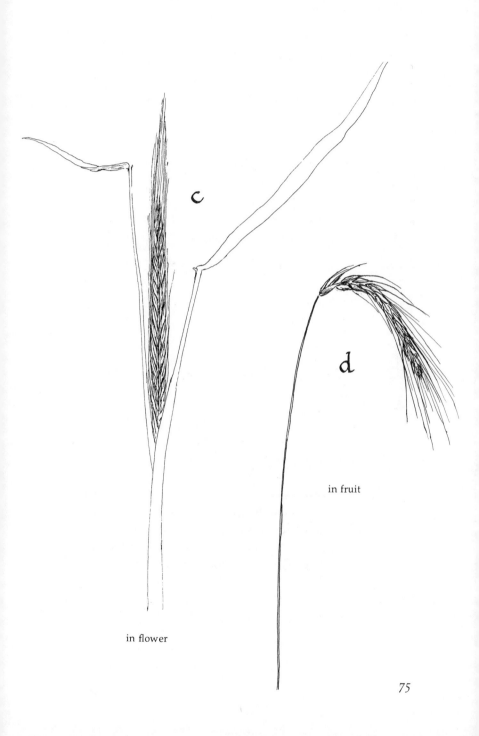

c

d

in fruit

in flower

Barley
Hordeum vulgare

Grass family   Gramineae

> flower clusters in groups of three
> long bristles; lower longer than upper
> inflorescence stays upright

60 cm–1.2 m (2–4 ft.)
alien
annual
occasionally spontaneous in fields or along
roadsides

Barley is an ancient crop, a staple in southern
Europe before the bread-making properties of
Wheat were discovered. Some Barley is grown for
human food but most of it is fed to animals or used
for malt. To make malt, the grain is sprouted under
carefully controlled conditions. Sprouting Barley
has a high content of the enzymes that are needed
to digest starch. When the sprouting has reached
the right stage, the plants are heated and dried. To
make beer, malt is mixed with other grains and the
enzymes in the malt turn the starches to sugar. The
next step is fermentation, which produces alcohol.

Barley requires roughly the same growing
conditions as Wheat — relatively cool and dry. It
cannot tolerate heat and humidity.

How to tell Wheat, Rye, and Barley apart:

These three agricultural grains can be hard to distinguish especially since there is much variation within each species, due to the presence of cultivated varieties. Remember these characteristics:

Wheat (p. 72) has fat round flower clusters. The flower clusters may or may not have bristles. The inflorescence is always upright.

Rye (p. 74) has long slender flower clusters. The flower clusters always have bristles. The edge of the flower scales has a tooth-like fringe. The inflorescence sometimes nods.

Barley has flower clusters more tapered than Wheat, but fatter than Rye. They may or may not have bristles. The bristles tend to be longer than those of Rye. The inflorescence may be upright or nod slightly.

c

b

a

d

Canada Wild Rye
Elymus canadensis

Grass family   Gramineae

a densely flowered, bushy
   inflorescence; usually straight,
   sometimes nodding
b bristles are coarse, thick, and
   curve outward
c single flower cluster; hard
   texture
d single flower
   relatively tall and coarse
   a good forage grass

usually grows in tufts 75 cm– 1.8 m
(2½–6 ft.)
dry or moist soil — dunes,
prairies, roadsides
native
perennial

Could be confused with
cultivated Rye, *Secale cereale*
(p. 74). Rye inflorescences
usually nod and all the bristles
are straight. *Elymus virginicus*
also has straight bristles.

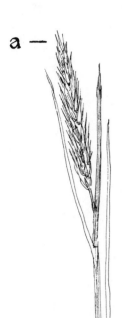

a —

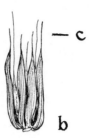

— c

b

Wild Rye
Elymus virginicus

Terrell Grass
Grass family   Gramineae

a stiff, upright, compact inflorescence
b single flower cluster; hard texture
c stiff straight bristles
    green; soon turns yellow
    good forage grass

30 cm–1.5 m (1–5 ft.)
grows in tufts
common along the edge of salt marshes; also
found in thickets and flood plains,
sometimes in prairies
native
perennial
June–October

Could be confused with Rye, *Secale cereale*
(p. 74), which has longer bristles, often
nods, and has a differently shaped flower
cluster. *Secale* is an alien annual that you
will find in fallow fields, along roads or
railroad tracks; these are not places where
you will find *Elymus*, which is a native
perennial.

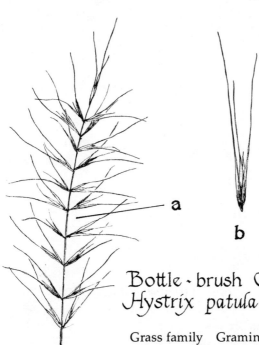

a

b

Bottle‑brush Grass
Hystrix patula

Grass family   Gramineae

a space between flower clusters varies
   considerably; sometimes flowers are
   closer together
b fairly large V-shaped flower clusters with
   long stiff bristles
   flowers fall off easily

medium-size: 60 cm–1.5 m (2–5 ft.)
woods
native
perennial
June–August

Could be confused with *Elymus virginicus*
(preceding), but *Hystrix* always has some
space between the flowers. *Hystrix* flowers
tend to point away from the stem, instead of
up, as in *Elymus*. Also, the flower
structures are different.

c

— a
— b

Sweet Vernal Grass
Anthoxanthum odoratum

Grass family   Gramineae

a inflorescence is fairly short, asymmetrical, papery textured

b very short branches; looks as if there are none

c reddish-green, then tan

small to medium-size: 20 cm–1 m (8 in–3½ ft.)

often fills whole fields, also grows along roadsides and in waste places

alien

perennial

a grass of early spring that usually disappears by midsummer

If it is crushed, or if you walk through a field of it, this grass has a strong unusual flavor. When I was little and wanted to chew on a piece of grass, I always unconsciously chose this one. Its flavor comes from a compound called coumarin, which is unpalatable to animals in large concentrations. If hay containing coumarin becomes spoiled, the coumarin is converted to a chemical that reduces blood clotting so that animals could bleed to death. However, coumarin is more of a problem with certain clovers than with *Anthoxanthum*. By itself, *Anthoxanthum* is too bitter for cows to eat, and its nutritive value is low, but it is sometimes mixed with other grasses for its flavor.

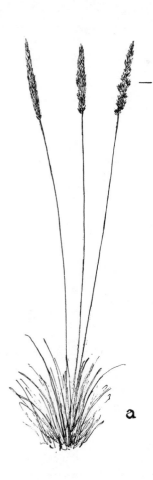

June Grass
Koeleria cristata

Grass family   Gramineae

a grows in bunches with narrow
 leaves at base, no leaves on stem
b dense narrow inflorescence, 3.8–
 15 cm (1½–6 in.) long
c single flower cluster — papery
d two lowest scales are as long as
 the others

small: less than 60 cm (2 ft.)
dry prairies, open woods — more
common toward the Midwest
native
perennial

Could be confused with *Festuca
ovina* or *F. rubra* (pp. 170–173) which
have more open inflorescences,
bristles on the flower scales, and the
two lowest scales of each flower
cluster shorter than the others.

Spike Grass
Distichlis spicata

Grass family   Gramineae

a chubby inflorescence
does not grow straight, but sprawls; forms dense mats

10 cm– 1.2 m (4 in.–4 ft.)
grows in salt marshes with *Spartina patens* (p. 128); covers
large areas
native
perennial
August–October

This species is unusual among the grasses in having the male
and female flowers on separate plants. The two look generally
similar except that the female inflorescences are usually fatter
than the male.

— a

b

Timothy
Phleum pratense

Herd's Grass
Grass family   Gramineae

a narrow cylindrical inflorescence;
rough-textured
b single flower
pale green, then tan

30 cm–1 m (1–3½ ft.)
very common in fields, roadsides
alien
perennial
early summer

Similar to *Alopecurus* (p. 88).

Timothy is a valuable grass for hay. In its growing state it is too rough to be eaten, but it dries well and makes a good winter food for livestock. From 1870–1910 it was a big cash crop because hay was needed to feed the horses that propelled the machines of the day. As gasoline-driven engines became common, the importance of Timothy in the nation's economy waned, but it is still widely planted.

There is some debate as to whether Timothy is native to this continent. The first record of it in this country is from 1711 when it was found growing wild by Jonathan Herd along the Piscataqua River in New Hampshire. It was assumed to be native, but the same species did exist at the same time in England, where it is called Cat's Tail. It is now thought that the seeds were brought over accidentally and the plants established themselves. The use of this grass for hay was first promoted in 1720 by a farmer named Timothy Hanson, whence the name Timothy.

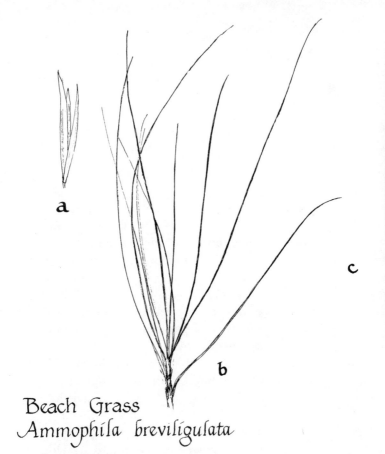

a

b

c

Beach Grass
Ammophila breviligulata

Sand Reed, Psamma, Marram
Grass family   Gramineae

a single flower
b basal leaves
c tall, stiff inflorescence; pale yellow, sometimes slightly
   purple
   inflorescence sticks up high above the narrow tufted leaves

up to 1 m (3½ ft.)
native
perennial
July–October

This is the common dune species that you see along the coast wherever there is sand. Even if you do not find the tall inflorescences, you have doubtless seen the tufts of basal leaves that trace circles in the sand as the wind blows about. *Ammophila* grows on the Atlantic coast down to Cape Fear, N.C. South of Cape Fear the Gulf Stream hugs the coast, causing warmer winters and a significant difference in plant species. It also grows along the shores of the Great Lakes.

Ammophila is valuable as a sand binder. The plants spread by long rhizomes and stolons and thus form a network that keeps the sand from blowing away. The plants also have the ability to keep on growing even though partly buried by sand.

Ammophila was much admired by Timothy Dwight, the famous early New England preacher and president of Yale College. He saw it growing in Provincetown, Massachusetts, when he traveled there in 1800, and considered it a sure manifestation of "the wisdom and goodness of the Creator."

"But for this single, unsightly vegetable," he wrote, "the slender barrier which here has so long resisted the ravages of the ocean had not improbably been long since washed away. In the ruins, Provincetown and its most useful harbor must have been lost; and the relief which the harbor and the inhabitants furnish to multitudes of vessels in distress . . . must have been prevented."

In a neighboring town, Truro, the inhabitants were required by law to plant *Ammophila,* in a crisscross pattern, "to shut up the interstices." However, Dwight noted that this regulation did little good, for the inhabitants then sent their cows out to graze on the dunes, which decimated the plants.

Ammophila breviligulata is still widely planted as a sand binder, both on the east and west coast of the United States. A European species, *A. arenaria,* is also planted and has been used to stabilize dunes in northern Europe for hundreds of years.

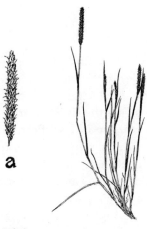

Foxtail
Alopecurus spp.

Grass family   Gramineae

a narrow cylindrical inflorescence,
soft to the touch
fields, waste places, shallow water, ditches

Grows in tufts low to the ground. Although it can grow up to
1 m (3½ ft.), it is usually much smaller. One species,
A. geniculatus, grows in sprawling mats with the stems lying
close to the ground.
Five species in our range, quite similar. Two are native, three
alien. Two are annual, three perennial.
April–September

Could be confused with Timothy (p. 84). *Alopecurus* is usually
smaller and has a different growth habit; Timothy does not
grow in such weak-stemmed clumps. The inflorescence of
Timothy is rougher to the touch and not shiny. Timothy does
not usually grow in damp soil. *Alopecurus* could also be
confused with *Setaria* (p. 68). The *Setaria* inflorescence is less
dense, as it consists of hard round grains, each with a tuft of
stiff bristles.

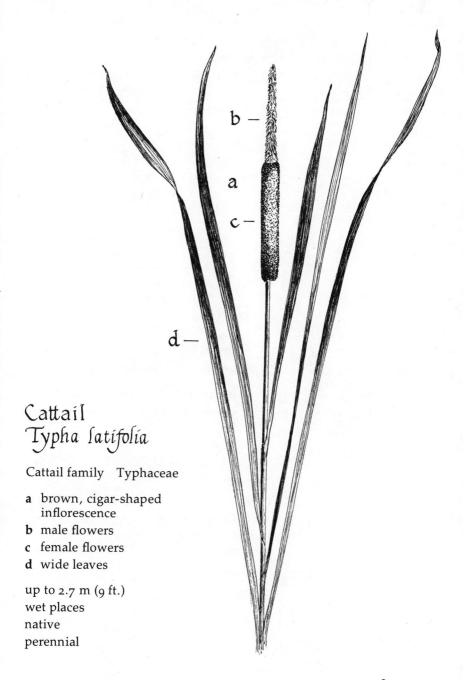

b —

a

c —

d —

Cattail
Typha latifolia

Cattail family   Typhaceae

a brown, cigar-shaped
  inflorescence
b male flowers
c female flowers
d wide leaves

up to 2.7 m (9 ft.)
wet places
native
perennial

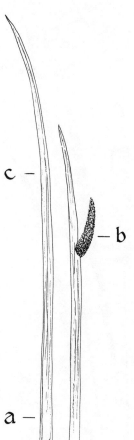

Sweetflag
Acorus calamus

Flagroot, Calamus
Arum family   Araceae

a leaves stiff, often red at base
b inflorescence (perfect flowers)
c leaves sharply folded
   spreads by rhizomes
   freshly broken leaves have a strong,
   spicy smell

up to 1 m (3½ ft.)
often grows in big patches in
wet places
native
perennial

Rhizomes used to make candy.

Common Plantain
Plantago major

Whiteman's Foot
Plantain family   Plantaginaceae

a broad basal leaves with prominent veins
b flowers extend most of the way down the stalk

up to 50 cm (20 in.)
a very common weed of lawns and roadsides; grows halfway
around the world
annual or perennial
June–October

This plant followed the settlers from Europe. The Indians felt
that it sprang up wherever the white man traveled, since he
created its preferred habitat, whence the name Whiteman's
Foot.

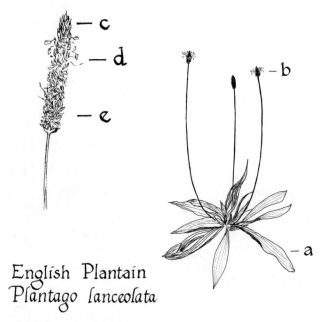

English Plantain
Plantago lanceolata

Ribgrass, Buckhorn
Plantain family   Plantaginaceae

a relatively narrow basal leaves with prominent veins
b flowers at top of stalk
c buds
d flowers
e dried remains

up to 75 cm (2½ ft.)
common weed of lawns and waste places
alien
annual

a

Quack Grass
Agropyron repens

Witch Grass, Couch Grass
Grass family   Gramineae

a flat flower cluster has two scales of
  equal length at the bottom
b no branches
c flower clusters have their backs
  toward the stem

medium-size: 30 cm–1.2 m (1–4 ft.)
common on roadsides and in meadows
native
perennial

Used for grazing and hay production,
but also can be a troublesome weed.

This is a widespread and important
genus. *Agropyron smithii* is one of the
principal grasses of the short-grass
prairie. The genus is closely related to
Wheat (*Triticum aestivum*) and it is
thought that perhaps Wheat as we
know it developed from a natural
hybrid with species of *Agropyron*.

93

a

b

c

English Rye Grass (not a true Rye)
Lolium perenne

Darnel
Grass family   Gramineae

a flower cluster has one big scale, bigger
than the others, on the side away from
the stem (this is not true for the top
flower cluster)
b flat flower clusters are placed sideways in
relation to the stem
c stem curves in and out and flower
clusters rest inside each curve

medium-size: 30–60 cm (1–2 ft.)
fields and roadsides — often planted as a
pasture grass or to stabilize soil after
construction
alien
short-lived perennial
May–August

Agropyron (preceding) and *Lolium* are hard
to tell apart unless you look closely.
Agropyron has flower clusters with their
back against the stem; *Lolium* flower clusters
are placed sideways to the stem. *Lolium*
flower clusters have one big scale at the base
(except for the terminal cluster); *Agropyron*
flower clusters have two equal-sized scales.

Paspalum spp.

Grass family   Gramineae

a flat, round seeds lined along one side
 of the stem
 may or may not have branches

grows in tufts, often sprawling, up to 1 m
(3½ ft.) tall
dry or moist areas, especially common in
sandy soil
most species native
some annual, some perennial

There are several species in this genus
that are quite similar.

Prairie Three-awn
Aristida oligantha

Whitegrass, Wiregrass, Needlegrass, Triple-awned Grass
Grass family   Gramineae

a three long bristles on each flower, slightly twisted at the
base

30–60 cm (1–2 ft.)
Grows low to the ground in dry sterile soil, often in large
masses. When mature, the plants turn a stark white, and you
can recognize a clump of it even from a distance by its
bleached-out appearance.
native
annual
late summer or fall: August–October

As the vernacular name implies, this species is common on the
prairie, but it also grows in the eastern states, mainly along
railroad tracks. On the prairie, it is an indicator of overgrazed
rangeland. Most prairie species are perennial and form a
dense sod that makes it impossible for annual species, such as
this one, to germinate. However, if the perennial species are
grazed too close, they will lose vigor and die, leaving open
space for the *Aristida* to come in. This process is accelerated
by the fact that cattle do not like *Aristida* because of the
bristles. So they leave it alone and continue to eat what is left
of the perennials, further weakening them. Soon, the *Aristida*
is dominant and the land is useless for grazing.

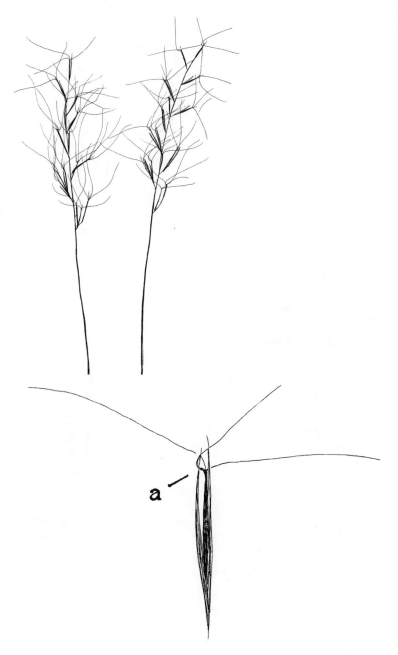

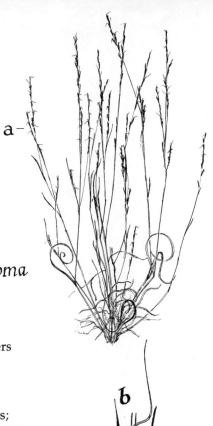

Poverty Grass
Aristida dichotoma

Grass family   Gramineae

a small bristles stick out
   horizontally from flowers
b single flower
   wiry
   often dark red
   flowers not conspicuous;
   whole plant inconspicuous
   except that it often covers large
   areas of dry ground

small: 3.8–48 cm (1½–16 in.)
grows in tufts in dry, poor soil
native
annual
late summer or fall: August–October

The common name for the genus *Aristida* is Three-awn (an
awn is a bristle). This particular species does not have three
conspicuous awns, but if you look closely at a single flower,
you will see that two of the awns are very small.

  Easily confused with *Sporobolus vaginiflorus* (p. 181) which
also grows in low tufts in dry soil. *Sporobolus* does not have
horizontal bristles.

– a

Sandbur
Cenchrus longispinus

Burgrass
Grass family   Gramineae

a horrible spiny flower clusters,
extremely painful to step on
usually low to the ground

less than 90 cm (3 ft.)
beaches, sandy soil
native
annual
July–October

A similar species, *C. tribuloides,* growing
south from Staten Island, has rounder,
very woolly flower clusters.

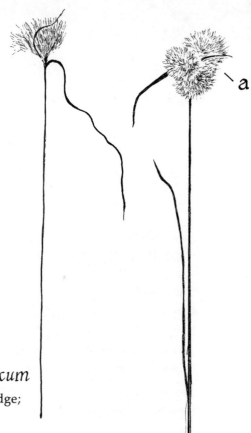

Cotton Grass
Eriophorum virginicum
(not a true grass, but a sedge;
also not related to
commercial cotton)

Bog Cotton
Sedge family   Cyperaceae

a fluffy clusters of white or tawny hairs
b single fruit

45 cm–1.2 m (1½–4 ft.)
bogs and peaty places
native
perennial

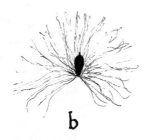

There are many other species in this genus, most of them more common northward. *Eriophorum* covers large areas of the tundra.

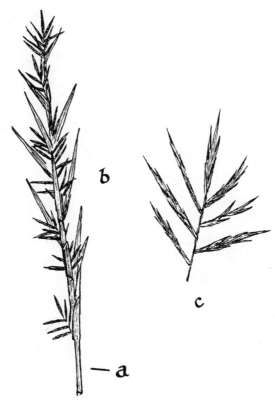

Three~way Sedge
Dulichium arundinaceum

Sedge family   Cyperaceae

a hollow leafy stem
b short leaves in three distinct rows
c flowers in flat clusters

20 cm–1 m (8 in.–3½ ft.)
wet places
native
perennial
July–October

Mountain Rice
Oryzopsis asperifolia

Grass family   Gramineae

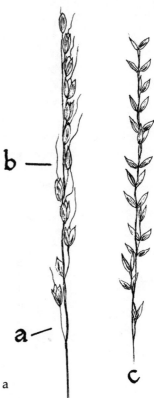

grows in low, leafy tufts
a short upright branches
b single oval flower cluster with a
   bristle that soon falls off
c empty scales left after grains have
   fallen out

5–12.5 cm (2–5 in.)
woods, thickets, and fields
native
perennial
spring flowering

This plant is not related to cultivated rice, *Oryza sativa*. Its
Latin name reflects an imagined relationship rather than a real
one because it comes from two words — *Oryza*, "rice," and
opsis, "appearance." This species does not even look much
like cultivated Rice, but the grains of some of the other species
in this genus do.

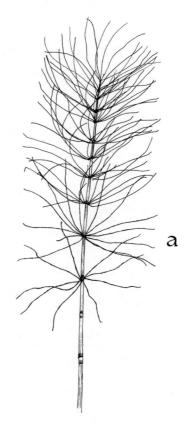

a

Horsetail
Equisetum arvense
(*equus* means "horse" in Latin and *seta* means "bristle")

Horsetail family   Equisetaceae

a "leaves" arranged in circles
around the stem
rough, wiry
up to 1 m (3½ ft.)
many habitats
native
perennial

These plants absorb silica, which gives them their rough
texture. They have been used as scouring brushes.

Gama Grass   *Tripsacum dactyloides*
(*dactyloides* comes from the Greek word for "finger")

Sesame Grass
Grass family   Graminae

a after flowering
b wide, cornlike leaves
c stigmas purple
d male flowers
e stamens orange
f female flowers
g in flower
   excellent forage grass

tall: 1–2.4 m (3½–8 ft.)
Grows in pure stands (not mixed with other plant species) in prairie lowlands; in the East you find it along the edge of salt marshes or woods, sometimes along roadsides. Does not grow in northern areas.
native
perennial

This grass is unusual in having separate male and female flowers. One of the few other grasses with this feature is Corn, *Zea mays* (p. 206). As far as we know, Corn is not a naturally occurring plant. It does not grow wild, nor does anything like it. It is the product of centuries of plant breeding on the part of the Central American Indians, but what it was bred from, we do not know. The search for the ancestor of Corn has been the subject of intense activity and debate, and for a while, the honor was bestowed on *Tripsacum*. This theory has been refuted, however, on the grounds that there is very little genetic similarity between *Tripsacum* and Corn. *Tripsacum* grows wild near countless cornfields and the two have never been known to hybridize in the wild.

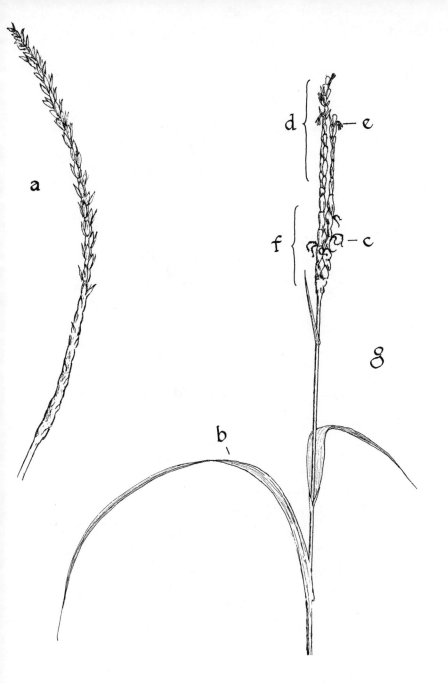

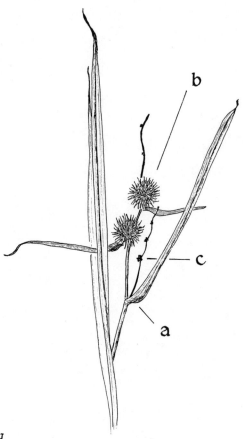

Bur - reed
Sparganium spp.

Bur-reed family   Sparganiaceae

a stiff upright leaves, bulging at the base
b female inflorescence: round, hard, bur-like
c shriveled male inflorescences

up to 1 m (3½ ft.)
wet places
native
perennial

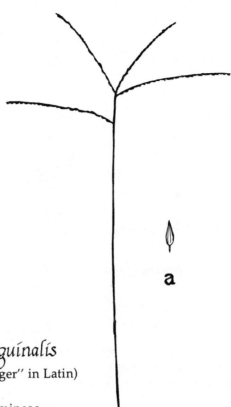

a

Crab Grass
Digitaria sanguinalis
(*digitus* means "finger" in Latin)

Grass family   Gramineae

a smooth oval seeds
   sprawling growth habit

0.3–1.2 m (1–4 ft.)
waste places, lawns, and gardens
alien
annual
June–October

This is the most unpopular weed of lawns and gardens, but
one that is likely to continue to flourish. A lawn is its
preferred habitat, and as we create the ideal conditions for
Digitaria, we must expect to find it growing in our yards.

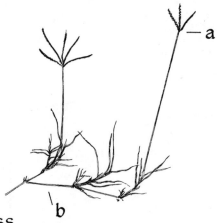

Bermuda Grass
Cynodon dactylon
(*dactylon* is from the Greek for "finger")

Scutch Grass, Wire Grass
Grass family   Gramineae

a flower stalks radiate like fingers
b crawls along by stolons
   low to the ground; forms mats

10–30 cm (4 in.–1 ft.)
yards, fields, waste places
alien
perennial

Introduced as a lawn grass, this species has become a troublesome weed in the South.

Easily confused with Crab Grass, *Digitaria sanguinalis* (preceding), which is generally bigger. *Digitaria* crawls, but it is an annual, so it does not form dense mats the way *Cynodon* does but instead tends to sprawl on top of the ground. Both have small oval-pointed seeds but *Cynodon* has two scales below each seed which stick out, giving the flowering branch a somewhat zigzag outline.

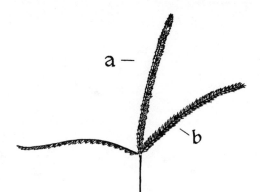

a —

b

Goose Grass
Eleusine indica

Yard Grass, Crab Grass, Wire Grass
Grass family   Gramineae

a toothed, jagged flower clusters
b flower branch looks like a closed zipper
    grows in tufts

30–60 cm (1–2 ft.)
yards and waste places
alien
annual
July–October

Easily confused with Crab Grass, *Digitaria sanguinalis* (p. 107),
but *Digitaria* has a different growth habit, does not have the
jagged flower clusters.

Big Bluestem
Andropogon gerardi

Beardgrass, Turkey Claw
Grass family   Gramineae

a inflorescence
b single flower
c coarse, slightly fuzzy flower
  branches radiating from the
  top of the stem
d leafy stem

tall: 75 cm–1.5 m (2½–5 ft.)
grows in clumps
native
perennial
late summer: August–October

Like the other *Andropogons,* this species presents a constantly
changing display of colors. In flower, the inflorescence varies
from bronze to a steely gray-blue; later the whole plant turns
shades of red, brown, and purple.

  Andropogon gerardi was the dominant species of the tall-
grass prairie. It is an excellent forage plant, and livestock
choose it over many other species. Although most of its
acreage has been plowed under, it still grows here and there in
the Midwest and the East — in dry open places, along
roadsides and shores, and in fields and prairies.

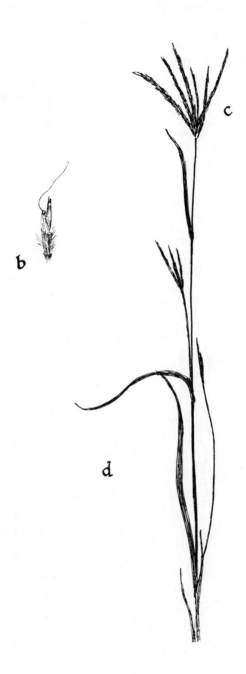

The Rush family: Juncaceae

The Rush family is a small one, with about 400 species world-wide. (The Grass family has 10,000; the Sedge family 4,000.) Most of the rushes grow in damp cool areas. In their flower structure, they are more like lilies than grasses (see p. 227).

The biggest genus in our area is *Juncus*. The different species of *Juncus* are not at all easy to tell apart, for the distinguishing features are small and there is considerable variation within each species. However, the following are some common species that you should be able to recognize fairly easily.

Path Rush

young plant

growing in a field;
straight and tall

d

Path Rush
Juncus tenuis

Rush family   Juncaceae

a usually grows in clumps
b tough stems
c curly bracts longer than the
       inflorescence
d three-parted capsule

6 mm–60 cm (¼ in.–2 ft.)
native
perennial; hard to pull up
June–September

growing in a parking lot;
tight scraggly clumps

As the name implies, this plant is often found on paths, both
in woods and in fields, where the soil is constantly packed
down. For this reason, you also see it in pastures and dirt
parking lots. It is not limited to these areas, however, but also
grows in fields, thickets, and swamps. It grows over the
entire American continent, in Europe, and North Africa.

Could be confused with *J. canadensis* (p. 116) which has
round leaves, a short bract, and flowers always in clusters, and
J. gerardi (next) which grows in salt marshes.

Black Grass
Juncus gerardí

(not a grass, but a member of the
Rush family)

Rush family   Juncaceae

a bracts shorter than inflorescence
b fruit
c sepals and petals
    in flower, the stamens are a
    bright magenta

15–75 cm (6 in.–2½ ft.)
grows in salt marshes; large patches
of it will often look brown from a
distance
native
perennial

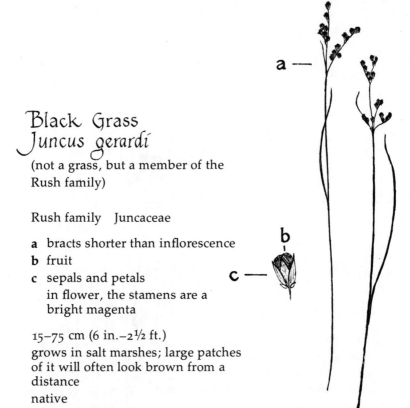

Similar to *Juncus tenuis* (preceding) but the bracts of *J. tenuis*
are longer than the inflorescence, those of *J. gerardi* shorter.
In *J. tenuis,* the sepals and petals are longer than the capsule,
making the fruit look bristly. In *J. gerardi,* the sepals and
petals are shorter so that the fruits look plump and round.
J. gerardi only grows in salt or brackish marshes, *J. tenuis* never
in such places.
    The coastal salt marshes were important to the early
colonists as sources of hay, and *Juncus gerardi* was a preferred
species. Although it is not a dominant plant of the salt marsh,
another species, *J. roemerianus,* is dominant further south.
J. roemerianus is much taller than *J. gerardi,* and has round
sharp-pointed leaves.

114

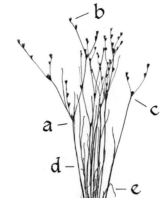

Toad Rush
Juncus bufonius

Rush family   Juncaceae

a branches start forking about
   halfway down the plant
b flowers relatively few on each
   branch; scattered
c no bracts (or very short ones)
   under inflorescence
d thin wiry stems
e short thin leaves
   easy to pull up since it is an
   annual

low to the ground: 3.8–35 cm (1½–14 in.)
damp open ground; roadsides
native
annual

This species grows almost all over the world.

Juncus canadensis

Rush family   Juncaceae

a leaves round
b faint horizontal rings around leaves (easier to see when plant is dry)
c fruit
d sepals and petals
e bract shorter than inflorescence
f flowers always in clusters
   thick-textured

wet places
native
perennial

A similar species, *Scirpus atrovirens* (p. 38), has a triangular stem and long leafy bracts under the inflorescence. *Juncus tenuis* (p. 113) has a bract longer than the inflorescence, does not have round leaves, and has flowers borne singly, not in clusters.

There are many species of *Juncus* quite similar to this one, distinguished on the basis of characteristics that are hard to see, such as the size and shape of the seed. This species varies considerably. It ranges greatly in size, 20 cm–1.2 m (8 in.–4 ft.). The inflorescence is sometimes widely spaced, with many forking branches; sometimes it is dense, with few branches. Sometimes the flower clusters form a sphere; sometimes not. Its constant characteristics are the round leaves with horizontal bands and the flowers in clusters. See p. 118 for information about galls on *J. canadensis*.

Gall on Juncus canadensis

A gall is a deformation of plant tissue caused when an insect lays its eggs on the plant. The larva lives inside the gall, using the plant for food and shelter. Certain species of insects always lay their eggs on certain species of plants and always cause the same kind of structure. Many galls have remarkable shapes that could easily be mistaken for a plant part.

This species of *Juncus,* as well as several others, is highly subject to gall formation, and a patch of it will often have more galled plants than normal ones. Cut the galls open and you might find some little insects. If you are at all interested in entomology, see if you can identify them and you will make a contribution to science. Only one published observation exists on the insect that forms these galls. A woman in 1916 noted adults of a sucking insect, *Livia maculipennis,* emerging from the Rush galls "in large numbers." However, one observation is not enough to become fact and the fact that these insects emerged from the gall does not necessarily mean that they caused it. For example, an insect that causes a gall in the first place is sometimes parasitized by other insects, who then take over the space. If you want to pursue this matter, Miss Patch's description appeared in the entomological journal *Pschye,* Vol. 23, No. 1, p. 21, 1916.

Livia maculipennis is in the order Homoptera, the plant-sucking insects, related to aphids, katydids, scale insects, and leafhoppers. *Maculipennis* means "spotted-wing."

a

b

Grass-leaved Rush
Juncus marginatus

Rush family   Juncaceae

a flowers in roundish clusters
b flat leaves (unlike many rushes which have round or
   channeled leaves)
   delicate
   papery texture

often small: less than 75 cm (2½ ft.)
moist soil
native
perennial

Similar to *Juncus canadensis*. The leaves are the best way to tell
these two apart. *J. canadensis* has round leaves with horizontal
bands, while *J. marginatus* has flat leaves. If you have a
specimen with no leaves, note that *J. marginatus* tends to be
more delicate, with round, thin-walled fruits. *J. canadensis*
fruits are thick and usually longer and narrower.

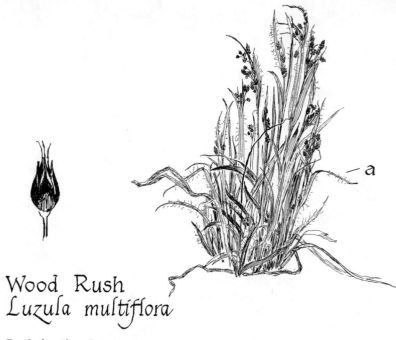

a

Wood Rush
Luzula multiflora

Rush family   Juncaceae

  flowers very early in the spring, before the leaves come out
  on the trees
a wispy white hairs scattered on stem and leaves
  red-brown color

small: less than 90 cm (3 ft.)
woods, fields, roadsides
native
perennial

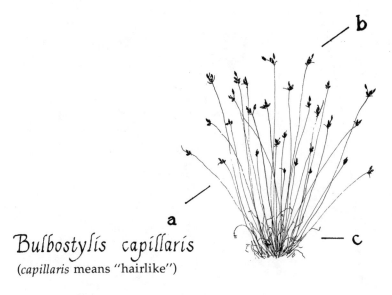

Bulbostylis capillaris

(*capillaris* means "hairlike")

Sedge family   Cyperaceae

a wiry stems — green, then brown or orange
b several flower clusters at top of stem
c wiry basal leaves

small: 2.5–40 cm (1– 16 in.)
grows in clumps in dry open soil
native
perennial
July–October

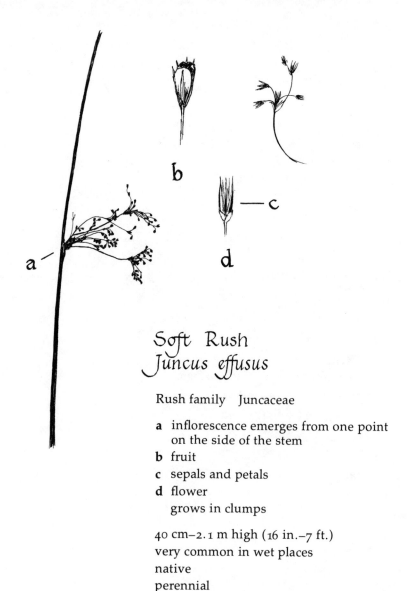

Soft Rush
Juncus effusus

Rush family   Juncaceae

a inflorescence emerges from one point
on the side of the stem
b fruit
c sepals and petals
d flower
grows in clumps

40 cm–2.1 m high (16 in.–7 ft.)
very common in wet places
native
perennial

Soft‑stem Bulrush
Scirpus validus

Great Bulrush
Sedge family   Cyperaceae

a stem green, round, easily
squashed
b inflorescence emerges from the
side of the stem; may have more
or fewer branches
grows in clumps

45 cm–3 m (1½–10 ft.)
wet places; fresh or brackish water
native
perennial

Juncus effusus and *Scirpus validus* could be confused, but the
flower structure of each is totally different. *Juncus effusus* has
three-parted capsules, each one borne singly at the end of a
branch. *Scirpus validus* has no capsules and the flowers are in
cone-shaped clusters.

Freshwater Cord Grass
Spartina pectinata

(*pectinata* means "comb-like," referring to the arrangement of the flowers on the branch)

Grass family   Gramineae

a stiff branches widely spaced
b flowers all lined on one side of the branch
c long thin leaves
d bristle on the end of flower scale

tall: 60 cm–2.1 m (2–7 ft.)
native
perennial
July–September

This is a common prairie grass, growing in spots that are too wet for grasses such as *Andropogon gerardi* and *Sorghastrum nutans*. Before the tall-grass prairie was plowed under, *Spartina pectinata* covered hundreds of square miles of the bottomlands on the Missouri River, often growing in pure stands (not mixed with other grasses). In the East, it occupies a different place in the landscape — you find it on the upland edge of salt marshes, where the soil is relatively dry. The grass has been used for hay.

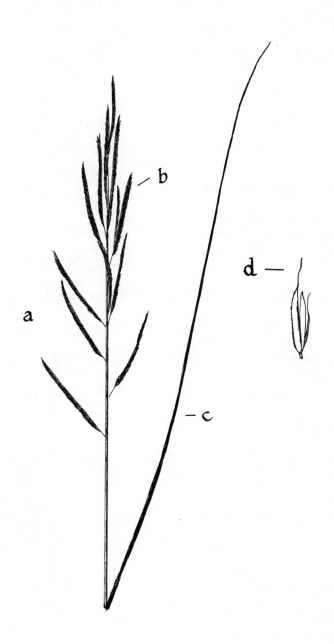

Salt Reed Grass
Spartina cynosuroides

Grass family   Gramineae

a flowers lined along one side
   of the branch
b no long bristle on the end
c single flower (flat)

tall: up to 3 m (10 ft.), and
stout
brackish or fresh tidal marshes
along the coast; not found
inland or north of Connecticut
native
perennial
August–October

Spartina pectinata (preceding)
and *S. cynosuroides* could be
confused until you have seen
both of them. Then the
differencenis clear, although it
is hard to verbalize. In
general, *S. cynosuroides* is
bigger and more robust. It has
a different range and habitat,
as it is not found inland or
north of Connecticut. It tends
to grow with its feet in the
water more often than
S. pectinata. If you're still not
sure of the difference, look at
the individual flowers.
S. pectinata flower scales have a
bristle on the end;
S. cynosuroides do not.

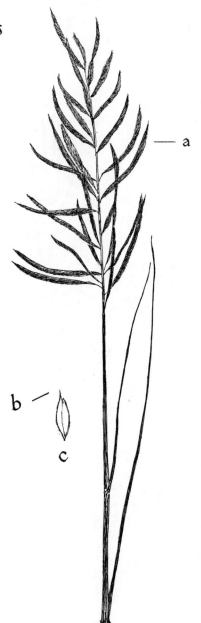

Saltwater Cord Grass, *Spartina alterniflora*

Grass family   Gramineae

a shaggy, tall, narrow inflorescence;
     almost appears to have no branches
b single flower (flat)
     yellow

tall: up to 2.4 m (8 ft.)
native
perennial
July–September

Spartina alterniflora is an important salt-
marsh species. In the Northeast you find
it growing along the outer edge of salt
marshes and along the edge of creeks and
ditches, where it is constantly flooded.
You also will find it growing on protected
beaches or on mud flats, and in these
situations it is acting as a colonizer,
initiating the formation of a salt marsh.
Once the plant gets started, it spreads by
rhizomes and builds a strong
underground network. As the plants
increase in density they trap silt and
cause the elevation of the soil to rise.
Other grass species, such as *Spartina
patens* (next) and *Distichlis spicata* (p. 83),
are more suited to a higher elevation, and
they will gradually replace the *Spartina
alterniflora*. These two are the dominant
grasses of a northeastern salt marsh.

In the Southeast, where the shore and
the tides are different, *S. alterniflora* is the
dominant salt-marsh species, covering
large areas.

Salt-meadow Cord Grass
Spartina patens

Grass family Gramineae

a thin stems and leaves
b flowers lined along one side of the
branch, like all species of *Spartina*
c single flower
does not grow upright; creeps along
stems bend easily and often form big
cowlicks in the salt marshes
flower scales purple at flowering time

small: less than 75 cm (2½ ft.)
salt marshes
native
perennial
late June–October

Without flowers, the leaves are easily confused with *Distichlis spicata* (p. 83).

When you look out over a salt marsh and see a large flat area covered with short grass, most of the grass is *Spartina patens.* It is normally flooded daily by salt water. Most plants would die immediately in such a situation, because the water would flow out of their cells in order to dilute the concentration of salt in the surrounding water. This phenomenon is called *osmosis,* where water moves through a membrane from a less concentrated solution to a more concentrated one. When the water flows out of a cell, the cell collapses.

Spartina has three adaptations that enable it to survive in this environment. First, it has a selective membrane in its roots that excludes much of the salt in the water. Second, it has special glands on its leaves that excrete salt water that does get in. Third, what little salt still remains is concentrated in the cells to counteract the osmotic pressure that would otherwise be exerted. This salt is mainly sodium chloride

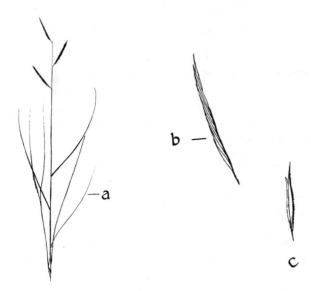

(table salt), the most prevalent salt in sea water. Unlike
animals, plants have little need for sodium chloride in their
physiological processes; nor does it disrupt these processes, so
they can afford to concentrate it. By these three mechanisms,
Spartina manages to survive in a difficult environment.

Nevertheless, its survival under these conditions is not
without cost. If you grow *Spartina patens* in a greenhouse,
watering it with fresh water, it will grow much bigger than the
plants on the salt marsh. It takes energy for the *Spartina* plant
to exclude salt water, energy that would otherwise produce a
larger plant. This example illustrates a common ecological
occurrence: plants that grow in severe environments (salt
marshes, deserts, mountaintops, and so forth) are often not
there because they grow best there, but because they are the
only plants that can grow there. They are there by default.

Little Bluestem, *Andropogon scoparius*

Broom Beardgrass, Prairie Beardgrass,
Broom, Wiregrass
Grass family   Gramineae

a fuzzy flowers lined along the branches
b wiry branches extend beyond the
leaves
c branches go most of the way down the
stem, intermingled with the leaves
d single flower cluster

45 cm–1.5 m (1½–5 ft.)
native
perennial
July–October

An important, widespread grass, this was
once the most abundant species in the
American mixed-grass prairie region.
Now that the prairie has been destroyed,
it is perhaps more common as an old-
field invader in the Northeast, although it
is still common in the Flint Hills area of
Kansas. Little Bluestem, as it is often
called, is an unfortunate name because
the plant is not little and it is only blue
(blue-green actually) when the shoots
first come up in the early summer — a
stage at which you are not likely to notice
it. By the time the flowering stalks come
out, it has turned a rich mixture of tan,
brown, and wine-red, and stays this way
through the winter. In dry soil such as
that along railroad tracks, it forms
definite clumps, but given more
moisture, it will form sod. It is an
excellent forage grass.

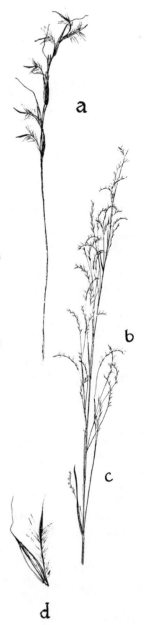

b

Broom Sedge
Andropogon virginicus
(not a true sedge)

Grass family   Gramineae

a flower stalks are tucked inside leaves
b silvery white hairs surrounding flower
tan yellow color
grows in clumps

50 cm–1.5 m (20 in.–5 ft.)
common in dry fields and along railroad
tracks
native
perennial
August–October

Andropogon scoparius (preceding) and *A. virginicus* could be
confused. *A. virginicus* is generally leafier, and the flowers are
tucked inside the leafy bracts. *A. scoparius* has longer flower
branches that stick out beyond the leaves.

Unlike its relatives, *A. scoparius* and *A. gerardi*, *A. virginicus*
is a poor forage grass and is a common invader on overgrazed
ranges. Because of its close resemblance to *A. scoparius*, some
land buyers have paid unreasonable prices for land covered
with *A. virginicus*, thinking they have bought good range.

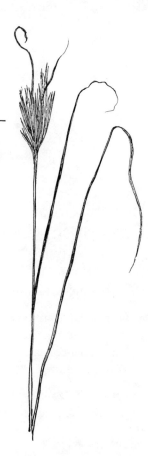

a —

Broom Sedge
Andropogon virginicus
var. abbreviatus

(not a true sedge)

Grass family   Gramineae

a leafy clump at the top of the stem
(the flowers are inside here)

medium size: 50 cm–1.5 m (20 in.–
5 ft.)
wet soil along the coastal plain
native
perennial
August–October

In the northern part of its range, this variety is completely
distinct from the typical *A. virginicus,* and has been called by
some a separate species — *A. glomeratus* (meaning "gathered
in bunches"). However, in the Southeast you will find
specimens intermediate between the two, so that it really
cannot be considered separate.

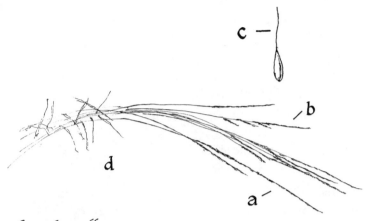

Nimblewill
Muhlenbergia schreberi

Drop-seed
Grass family   Gramineae

a inflorescence 6–19 cm (2½–7½ in.) long
b short branches that hug the stem; inflorescence is long and narrow
c short delicate bristle on each flower
d stems rarely grow straight up, but fall over and sprawl, often rooting at the nodes; usually grows in a sprawling mass
   shiny; green to purple

roadsides, doorways, thickets, gardens (can be a troublesome weed)
native
perennial

Reed
Phragmites communis
(*communis* means "growing in colonies")

Grass family   Gramineae

a stiff wide leaves
b coarse hollow stem
c big plumy inflorescence; purple in flower, gray in fruit
d flower cluster
    usually grows in large colonies, as it spreads by rhizomes

tall: up to 3.9 m (13 ft.)
ditches; ponds; fresh, alkaline or brackish water; edges of salt
marshes
native; distributed almost worldwide
perennial
July–September

A common and sometimes unpopular grass, *Phragmites* seems
to have been spreading in the Northeast with the general
increase of industrialization and urbanization. It often
invades salt marshes that have been filled, diked, or otherwise
altered. As such, it is a symptom, not a cause, of disturbance.
It spreads quickly by rhizomes and is resistant to all kinds of
disturbance. If it is cut or burned, it comes back more
vigorously than before. Some government and private
organizations are making great efforts to get rid of *Phragmites*,
but it seems futile.
    Phragmites has been used to make pen points. John Howard
Benson, a famous calligrapher, wrote that a *Phragmites* quill is
the best available. In the Soviet Union, *Phragmites* is used as a
source of cellulose for paper manufacture and is an important
crop.

135

Eulalia
Miscanthus sinensis

(*sinensis* means "Chinese")

Grass family   Gramineae

a big plumy inflorescence; white-gray hairs
b single branch
   grows in clumps

tall: up to 2.7 m (9 ft.)
This plant was brought over from eastern Asia to be grown as
an ornamental. It has escaped and manages occasionally to
grow on its own along roadsides and in old fields.
alien
perennial
September–November

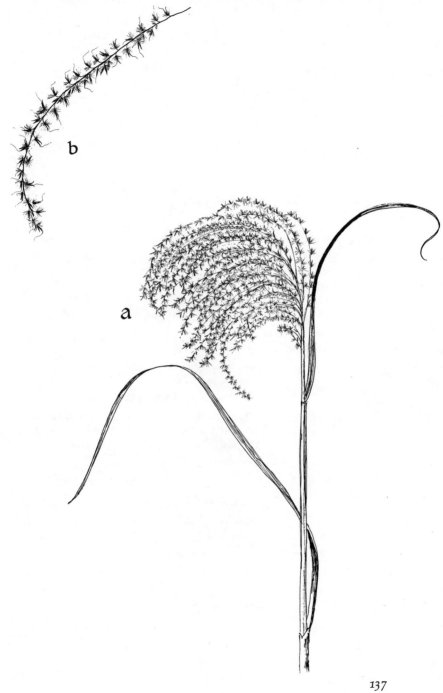

b

a

137

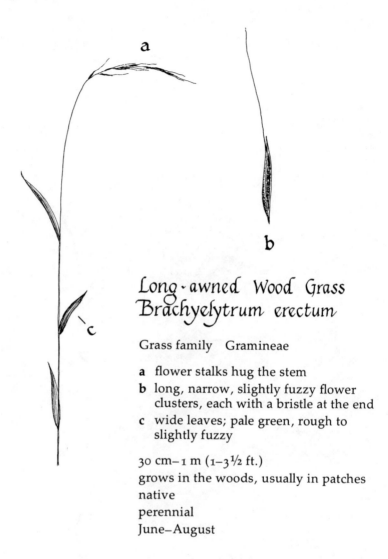

a

b

c

Long-awned Wood Grass
Brachyelytrum erectum

Grass family   Gramineae

a flower stalks hug the stem
b long, narrow, slightly fuzzy flower
   clusters, each with a bristle at the end
c wide leaves; pale green, rough to
   slightly fuzzy

30 cm–1 m (1–3½ ft.)
grows in the woods, usually in patches
native
perennial
June–August

a —

Tall Grama Grass
Bouteloua curtipendula

Mesquite Grass
Grass family   Gramineae

a short flower clusters hanging mainly
from one side of the stem

30 cm– 1 m (1–3½ ft.)
dry woods and prairies
native
perennial

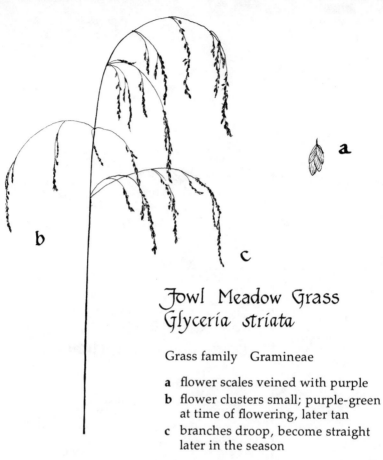

Fowl Meadow Grass
Glyceria striata

Grass family   Gramineae

a flower scales veined with purple
b flower clusters small; purple-green at time of flowering, later tan
c branches droop, become straight later in the season

medium-size: 30 cm − 1.5 m (1–5 ft.)
common in wet places
native
perennial
mainly spring flowering, usually disintegrates by late summer

How to distinguish the species of *Glyceria*: *G. canadensis* has fat green flower clusters, drooping branches; stems are slender. *G. striata* has smaller flower clusters, usually purple; drooping branches; stems are slender. *G. grandis* has small flower clusters, usually purple; branches do not droop so severely; stems are fat.

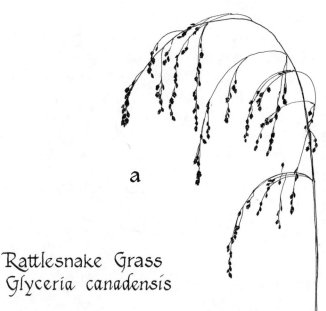

a

Rattlesnake Grass
Glyceria canadensis

Grass family   Gramineae

a drooping branches
b flower clusters fat and heavy;
   green

30 cm–1 m (1–3½ ft.)
wet places
native
perennial
July–August

For similar species, see preceding
account.

b

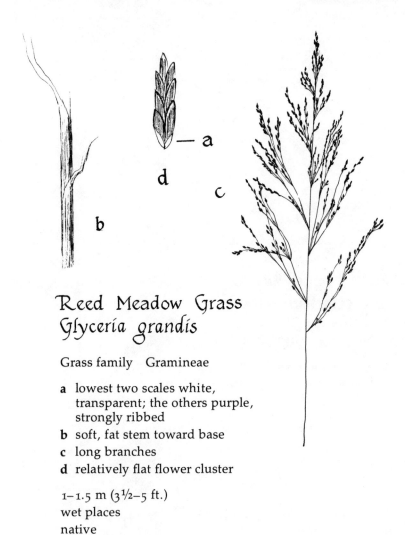

Reed Meadow Grass
Glyceria grandis

Grass family   Gramineae

a lowest two scales white, transparent; the others purple, strongly ribbed
b soft, fat stem toward base
c long branches
d relatively flat flower cluster

1–1.5 m (3½–5 ft.)
wet places
native
perennial

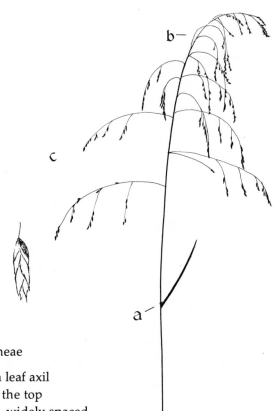

Purple - top
Triodia flava

Tall Redtop
Grass family   Gramineae

a little tuft of hairs in leaf axil
b stem sticky toward the top
c drooping branches, widely spaced
   spikelets red-purple at first, then turn brown

tall: 75 cm–2.1 m (2½–7 ft.)
dry fields, roadsides; not found in
northern New England
native
perennial
August–October

Could be confused with *Glyceria* spp. (pp. 140–142). *Glyceria*
has no tufts of hair in the leaf axils, is not sticky at the top.
Glyceria grows in wet places and flowers in the spring and
summer. *Triodia* grows in dry places and flowers in late
summer and early fall.

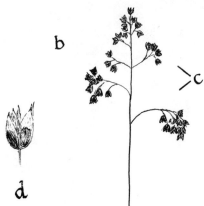

Holy Grass
Hierochloë odorata

Vanilla Grass (supposedly smells like vanilla)

Grass family   Gramineae

a   short stiff leaf
b   short inflorescence
c   some branches droop, some point
    upward
d   wide bell-shaped flower cluster
    shiny; tan, bronze, or purple

30–60 cm (1–2 ft.)
moist soil; edges of salt marshes and bogs
native
perennial
flowers in spring, then shrivels up

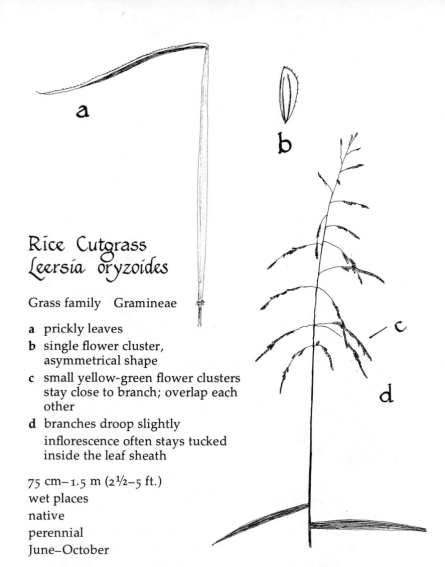

Rice Cutgrass
Leersia oryzoides

Grass family   Gramineae

a prickly leaves
b single flower cluster,
   asymmetrical shape
c small yellow-green flower clusters
   stay close to branch; overlap each
   other
d branches droop slightly
   inflorescence often stays tucked
   inside the leaf sheath

75 cm–1.5 m (2½–5 ft.)
wet places
native
perennial
June–October

Could be confused with *Poa* species (p. 191–196) but the
flowers are different. *Poa* flower clusters have several
overlapping scales. Nothing else cuts like *Leersia;* getting
caught in a patch of it with bare legs is an unpleasant
experience.

   This species is closely related to Rice (*Oryza sativa*) by virtue
of its flower structure.

Hair Grass
Deschampsia flexuosa

Grass family   Gramineae

a large tufts of straight, wiry basal leaves that last through the winter
b inflorescence is only on the upper part of the stem
c thin delicate branches fork at wide angles to each other
  flowers bronze or purple, then tan; shiny

30–75 cm (1–2½ ft.)
grows in clumps in sandy soil, in sun or thin shade
common in dry oak woods where the canopy is not thick
native
perennial
June–August

before flowering — green

Could be confused with *Agrostis perennans* and *A. hyemalis* (pp. 154–157). These have wider inflorescences that occupy a much greater proportion of the whole plant. Neither of them has such big tufts of basal leaves. *Deschampsia* has bigger flowers than *Agrostis*.

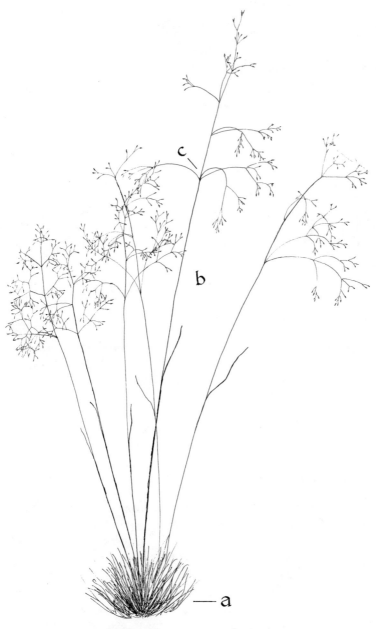

after flowering — orange to brown

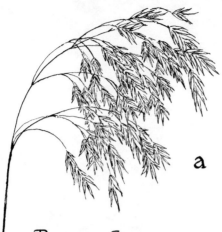

a

b

Brome Grass
Bromus ciliatus

Grass family   Gramineae

a branches droop to one side
b overlapping scales each with a short bristle at the
end
inside edge of scales fuzzy (a similar unillustrated
species, B. purgans, has fuzz over the entire scale)
flowers pale green, sometimes tinged with brown
or purple

30 cm–1.5 m (1–5 ft.)
woods and wood edges, thickets, rocky slopes
native
perennial
July–October

How to distinguish the different species of Bromus:
B. japonicus and B. tectorum tend to flower in the
spring, then disappear. They grow in waste places
and disturbed areas, not in the woods. They are
usually smaller than B. ciliatus. B. tectorum has
completely fuzzy flower scales; B. ciliatus' flower scales
are fuzzy only on the edge; B. japonicus' flower scales
are smooth and the flower clusters are heavy.

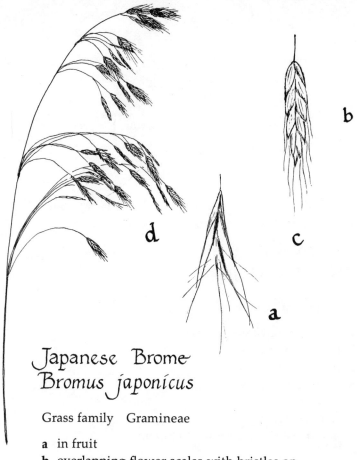

Japanese Brome
Bromus japonicus

Grass family   Gramineae

a in fruit
b overlapping flower scales with bristles on
    each one
c in flower
d flower clusters heavy; drooping
    fuzzy sheaths
    rattles a little if you shake it

grows to a height of 1 m (3½ ft.)
roadsides, waste places
alien
annual

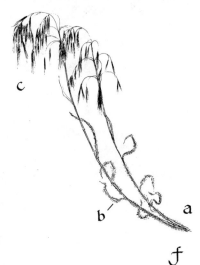

Downy Chess
Bromus tectorum

Grass family   Gramineae

a usually sprawls at the base
b leaves very fuzzy
c inflorescence droops
d fuzzy flower scales
e long bristles
f flowering: silvery gray, shining
g after flowering: wine-red to brown

usually grows low to the ground, but can grow as
high as 1 m (3½ ft.)
roadsides, waste places, beaches
alien
annual; common spring weed
May–June

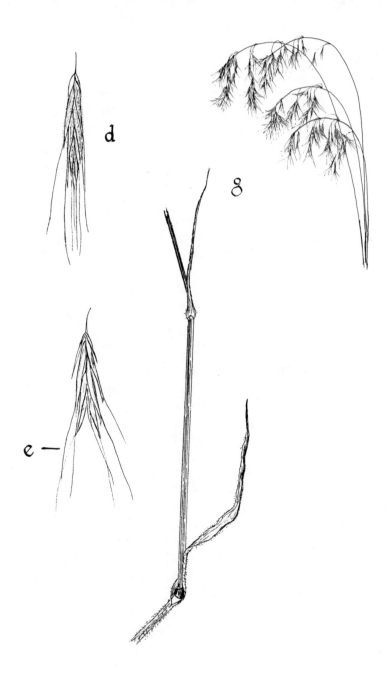

d

g

e —

Redtop
Agrostis alba

Bentgrass
Grass family   Gramineae

a branches in bunches
b flower cluster only has one flower
c very wispy and delicate; often shiny
d before flowers open
e in flower
   reddish-purple to green when flowering, then tan; stays tan
   through most of the summer

20 cm–1.2 m (10 in.–4 ft.)
long-lived perennial
usually a grass of late spring but can flower from June to
September

Very variable, both in the shape of the inflorescence and in
growth form. Sometimes the stems sprawl along the ground,
sending out many stolons, rooting at the nodes; sometimes the
plant grows in compact, distinct circular tufts. It could be confused with *Poa* (p. 191–196) or *Calamagrostis* (p. 201). *Poa* has
several overlapping scales in the flower cluster and has a boat-
shaped leaf tip. *Calamagrostis* grows more often in wet places
and has a little tuft of silky hairs at the base of each flower.

Agrostis alba is a sod-former, a grass that spreads by stolons
and forms a dense mat. Such a grass, of course, is good for
lawns and this is the main use for *Agrostis* today.

Agrostis is apparently native in the northern part of the
country, but it was also brought over by the Europeans to be
grown for hay and it spread quickly. You now find it in fields
and roadsides all across the continent, as well as in Europe,
Asia, and western Africa.

The name Redtop applies to its color while flowering, but it
is not too useful because the flowering period is a short
portion of the time that you see the plant.

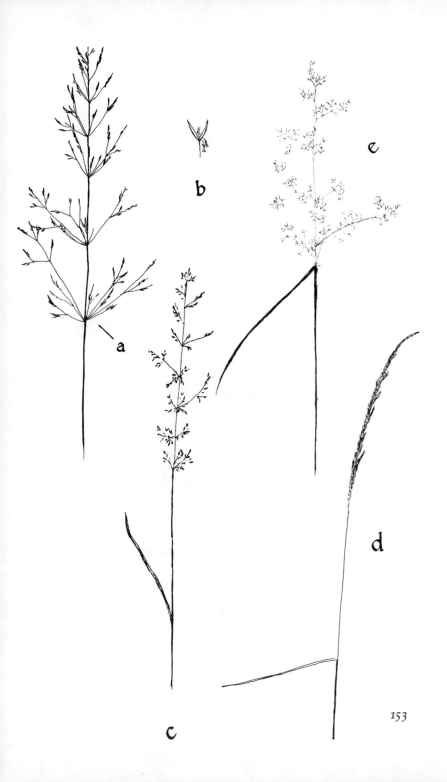

Upland Bent
Agrostis perennans

Thin Grass
Grass family   Gramineae

a grows in clumps; leafy at base
b large, wide inflorescence
   delicate branches
   flowers usually pale green, sometimes purple

30 cm– 1 m (1–3½ ft.)
woods and shaded areas; also dry or moist open soil
native
perennial
fall flowering: late July–October

How to distinguish the different species of *Agrostis: A. alba*
has the most narrow inflorescence of the three, and the
inflorescence is smallest in proportion to the whole plant.   In
A. perennans and *A. hyemalis* the inflorescence occupies a large
portion of the whole stem.   *A. perennans* and
A. hyemalis are generally bigger than *A. alba.   A. perennans*
and *A. hyemalis* could be more easily confused.   In general,
A. hyemalis has a wider, more wiry inflorescence than
A. perennans.   The branches are longer, and the flowers and
the secondary branches are toward the outer end.   The
secondary branches stay close to the main ones.   *A. hyemalis* is
usually purple or brown, *A. perennans* usually green.   The
leaves of *A. hyemalis* are more narrow and wiry than those of
A. perennans.

a

b

Ticklegrass
Agrostis hyemalis

Hairgrass
Grass family   Gramineae

a small shiny flower clusters at the ends of the branches
b long delicate branches that branch again toward the outer
  end
c inflorescence is wide and occupies most of the height of the
  plant
  narrow leaves at base
  grows in clumps
  branches rough if you run your fingers along them

up to 1 m (3½ ft.)
dry or moist open soil, thin woods, sandy areas, waste places
native
perennial
A. hyemalis flowers only from May to June but an almost
identical species, *A. scabra*, flowers from June to November.

The inflorescence is at first green-purple and shining, then
tan. After flowering, the inflorescence often breaks off and
floats around like a tumbleweed.

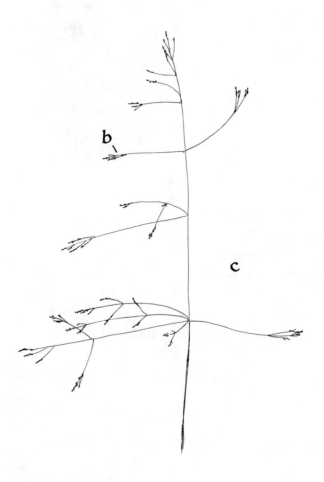

Eragrostis pectinacea

Grass family   Gramineae

  thin delicate branches
  flower clusters lead-colored
  thin, flat flower clusters

grows in sprawling tufts
small: 5–75 cm (2 in.–3½ ft.)
waste places, common in cracks of city sidewalks
annual
native
July–October

The genus Panicum

The genus *Panicum* (Panic Grass) is a large, confusing one. In the Northeast it contains 75 species; many look quite similar and vary considerably in the obvious characteristics that one would like to use to tell them apart. The genus as a whole is distinguished by small oval flower clusters borne singly at the end of the branches. The inflorescence usually has many branches. Most of the species are perennial, and these are the hardest to tell apart. The few annual species are mainly weeds, found around civilization, and they are relatively easy to identify.

Among the perennial species, a large group has an unusual life cycle. They have basal rosettes of leaves that stay green through the winter. In the early part of the season, anywhere from April to August, they send up a conspicuous terminal flowering shoot. Later in the season the plant starts branching profusely and produces small inflorescences tucked in the leaf axils. These flowers never open but instead pollinate themselves.

Of the species illustrated here, *P. clandestinum* and *P. lanuginosum* fall into this group. *P. capillare* and *P. dichotomiflorum* are annuals. *P. virgatum* is a perennial but it does not have overwintering basal leaves and does not produce the second round of self-pollinating flowers.

How to distinguish the different species of *Panicum*: *P. clandestinum* has stiff wide leaves, and a relatively small, unbranched inflorescence. *P. lanuginosum* is small and grows in tufts with basal evergreen leaves. *P. dichotomiflorum* has fat stems, a large much-branched inflorescence, and no hairs. *P. capillare* has a large, delicate, much-branched inflorescence and very fuzzy leaf sheaths. *P. virgatum* grows in big leafy clumps and has no hairs.

Species of *Panicum* could also be confused with *Eragrostis spectabilis* (p. 167) or *Leptoloma cognatum* (p. 168). All species of *Panicum* have rounded, oval-shaped flower clusters. *Eragrostis* flower clusters are flat, with several overlapping flower scales. *Leptoloma* has tufts of hairs in the axils of the flower branches and a brittle inflorescence that snaps off easily.

a

Switch Grass
Panicum virgatum

Grass family Gramineae

   grows in big leafy clumps
a no evergreen leaves at base
b flowers are borne singly at the
   ends of the branches; grain is
   hard and bony
c inflorescence 5–50 cm (2–20
   in.)
   purple in flower, then tan

up to 2.1 m (7 ft.)
native
perennial

This is another common grass of the tall-grass prairie, growing
in relatively wet areas as a sod-former. It is a good forage
species and is often planted. Specialized strains have been
developed by breeders to grow in different conditions.

   In the East you find Switch Grass more often in dry soils —
along sandy roadsides and along the upland edge of salt
marshes, and it grows in bunches. The leafy clumps last
through the winter, though dead, and their yellow color
provides a touch of brightness on dark rainy days.

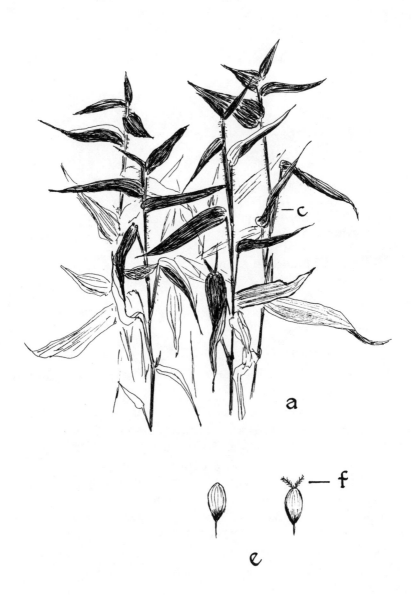

a

c

e

f

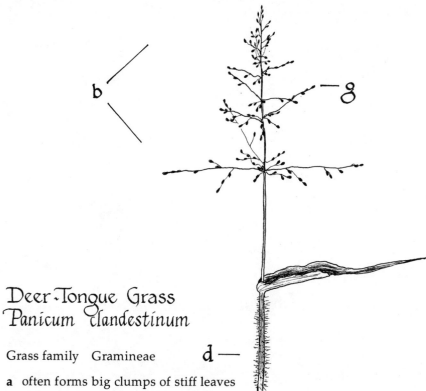

Deer-Tongue Grass
Panicum clandestinum

Grass family   Gramineae

a often forms big clumps of stiff leaves
b inflorescence 7.5–15 cm (3–6 in.)
c leaf sheath pulls conspicuously away from the stem
d rough hairs (usually)
e single flower
f stigmas
g small oval flowers at the end of the branches

flowering stalks as high as 1.5 m (5 ft.) but usually smaller
thickets, edges of woods, shores, waste places, gardens (often
a troublesome weed)
native
perennial

The flowering stalks appear from May to September, but lose
the flowers rapidly. The leaf masses persist through the
winter.

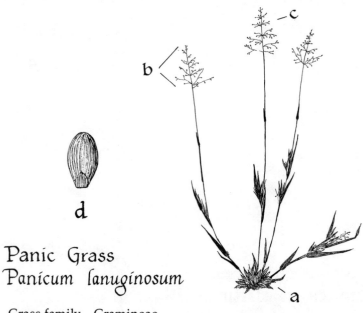

Panic Grass
Panicum lanuginosum

Grass family   Gramineae

a short wide basal leaves in a tight clump; last through the winter
b inflorescence 3.8–12.5 cm (1½–5 in.)
c small oval flower clusters at the end of each branch
d single flower
  very variable

15 cm–1 m (6 in.–3½ ft.)
moist or dry soil; thin woods; dunes, shores; prairies
native
perennial

For similar species, see p. 159.

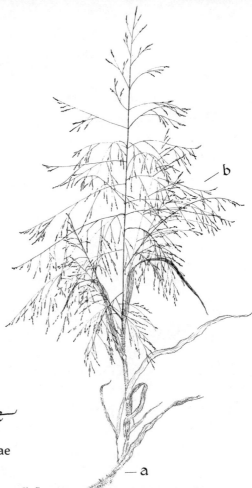

b

a

Old Witch Grass
Panicum capillare

Grass family   Gramineae

a very hairy
b many fine branches; small flowers
huge inflorescence, almost as big as the whole plant, up to
40 cm (16 in.)
inflorescence breaks off and floats around like a
tumbleweed
often purple at flowering time

grows in dry sandy or stony soil or as a weed in fields
native
annual
late summer: July–October

For similar species, see p. 159.

Fall Panicum
Panicum dichotomiflorum

Grass family   Gramineae

a smooth flat stem
b relatively wide leaves
c many branches
   inflorescence green or purple, up to 40 cm (16 in.) long
   often grows in sprawling clumps

up to 2.1 m (7 ft.) tall
roadsides, waste places; common in cities
native
annual; easy to pull up
usually does not appear till late summer

For similar species, see p. 159.

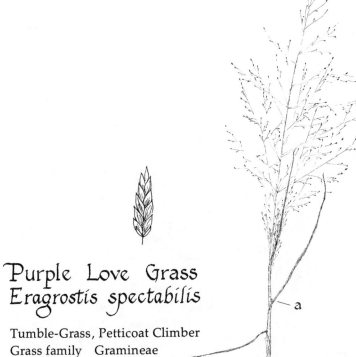

Purple Love Grass
Eragrostis spectabilis

a

Tumble-Grass, Petticoat Climber
Grass family   Gramineae

a tufts of hair in the axils
inflorescence purple, then tan; stiff, delicate
flower cluster flat; overlapping scales
grows low to the ground in little tufts

20–45 cm (8–18 in.)
common in sandy soil
native
perennial

Could be confused with *Leptoloma cognatum* (next) or *Panicum*
(p. 159).

A beautiful grass of late summer and early fall that forms
clouds of purple along the side of the road. After flowering,
the inflorescence breaks off and floats around like a
tumbleweed.

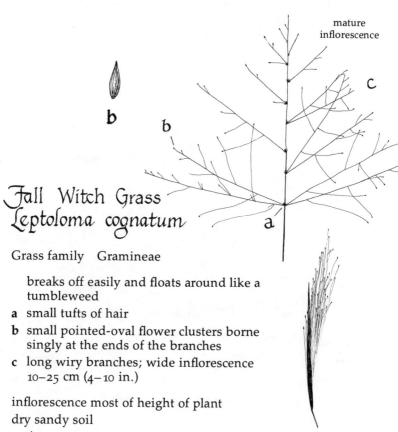

mature
inflorescence

b

b

c

Fall Witch Grass
Leptoloma cognatum

a

Grass family   Gramineae

breaks off easily and floats around like a
tumbleweed
a small tufts of hair
b small pointed-oval flower clusters borne
singly at the ends of the branches
c long wiry branches; wide inflorescence
10–25 cm (4–10 in.)

inflorescence most of height of plant
dry sandy soil
native
perennial
June–October

young shoot

Easily confused with *Eragrostis spectabilis*
(preceding) which has a flat flower cluster of
several overlapping scales. Could also be
taken for *Panicum*; see p. 159.

Although it grows low to the ground, this
can be a conspicuous grass. When ripe, the
whole inflorescence is purple-pink and a
patch of it forms a colored mist noticeable
even from a distance.

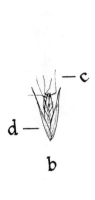

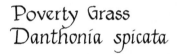

Poverty Grass
Danthonia spicata

Junegrass, White Oat Grass
Grass family   Gramineae

a always grows in clumps with wiry
   stems naked for much of their length
b flower clusters relatively transparent, delicate
c short bristles going in different directions
d two lowest scales longer than the whole flower cluster
e short branches in the inflorescence point upward
f basal tufts of curly leaves

medium-size: 10–60 cm (4 in.–2 ft.)
usually found in dry soil
native
perennial
flowers May–July, but basal leaves last through the year

Easily confused with *Festuca rubra* (p. 172). *F. rubra* has
straight basal leaves, not curly, and flower bristles are straight,
not crooked.

Sheep Fescue
Festuca ovina

(*ovina* means "of sheep")

Grass family   Gramineae

a grows in distinct tussocks with wiry blue-green basal leaves
b inflorescence stiff, with few branches; pale green or violet, then tan

short: less than 75 cm (2½ ft.)
dry soil; used for lawns in sandy areas
alien
perennial
flowers in May and June; the flowering stalks disintegrate but basal leaf tufts last through the year

F. ovina is often found as a pasture grass in hilly, rocky areas, where sheep graze.

   F. ovina and *F. rubra* can be very hard to tell apart. They are similar, but each one varies considerably. In general, *F. ovina* is smaller than *F. rubra* and the inflorescence occupies a smaller proportion of the plant. The inflorescence of *F. ovina* ranges from 3.8–10 cm (1½–4 in.); that of *F. rubra* from 2.5– 22.5 cm (1–9 in.). In general, the inflorescence of *F. ovina* is more narrow, but these characteristics are variable. The only constant features are the sheaths at the base of the stems, and these are hard to see. The basal sheaths of *F. ovina* are white and stay intact through the season. Those of *F. rubra* are red or brown and become shreddy and fibrous.

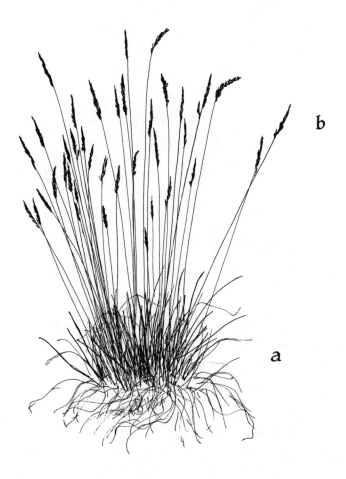

b

a

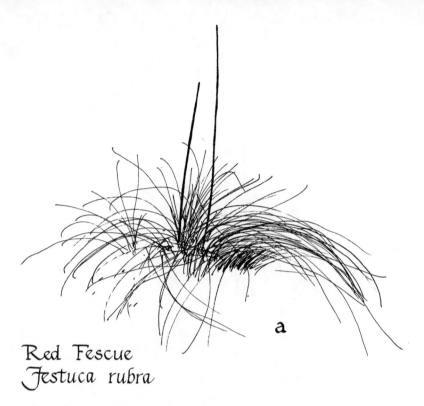

a

Red Fescue
Festuca rubra

Grass family   Gramineae

a round wiry basal leaves, dark at base
b stem leaf rolled at the edge
c no bulge at base of leaf
d flower cluster
e several overlapping scales, each one with a short bristle at
the end
  very variable, as shown

up to 90 cm (3 ft.)
grows in tufts in dry or rocky soil or in lawns
native
perennial

Although *F. rubra* grows naturally in the sun, it is valued as a
lawn grass for shady spots. Many cultivated varieties have
been developed.

Orchard Grass
Dactylis glomerata

(*glomerata* means "gathered in
bunches," referring to the arrangement
of the flowers)

Cock's Foot
Grass family   Gramineae

a short stiff side branches
b flowers in irregular rounded
    clusters; rough texture

medium-size: 45 cm–1.5 m (1½–5 ft.)
alien
perennial
May–September

This is a very common grass, seen
almost throughout the U.S. in fields,
waste places, and along roadsides. It
was brought over from Europe to be
cultivated as a forage grass. George
Washington wrote of it: "Orchard
Grass of all others is in my opinion the
best mixture with clover; it blooms
precisely at the same time, rises quick
again after cutting, stands thick, yields
well, and both cattle and horses are
fond of it green or in hay." It grows
well in rich or poor soils and in the
shade. It flowers naturally in the
spring but if mowed, it will grow back
vigorously and flower again.

Reed Canary Grass
Phalaris arundinacea

Grass family   Gramineae

a wide leaves
b single flower
c two scales about equal size; papery
d short branches
   inflorescence green or slightly purple at
   first, then becomes tan

tall: up to 2.1 m (7 ft.)
forms large colonies in wet places
native
perennial
May–August
inflorescence is open at the time of
flowering, then closes up
flowers mostly in spring but the dried inflorescences remain, overtopping the leaves

You might find an occasional *Phalaris* plant
growing upland that could be confused with
Orchard Grass (opposite). However, the
leaves of *Phalaris* are much wider, the
inflorescence more narrow and pointed, and
the individual flowers shaped differently.

A related species, *Phalaris canariensis*,
native to the Canary Islands, is a major
source of commercial bird food. The canary
bird also comes from the Canary Islands.

Phalaris makes a good hay, and lowland
meadows of it are often harvested. In spite
of the fact that it grows naturally in wet
places, it will do well if planted on an
upland site, and it often is.

(See next page for different form.)

Ribbon Grass
Phalaris arundinacea
forma variegata

Grass family   Gramineae

Sometimes in a plant population mutations appear that have
characteristics desirable for horticulture. The horticulturists
call these "sports," the botanists, "forms." Ribbon Grass is a
form of *P. arundinacea* (preceding) that is grown in gardens.

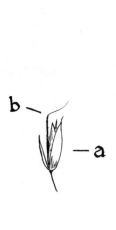

b

— a

c

Tall Oats Grass
Arrhenatherum elatius

Grass family   Gramineae

a papery scales
b twisted bristle
c inflorescence tall and narrow; silvery
   green at time of flowering; shining

1 m (3½ ft.) or more
roadsides, fields
alien
perennial
a grass of early summer (June–July)
which then disintegrates

Often grown for hay.

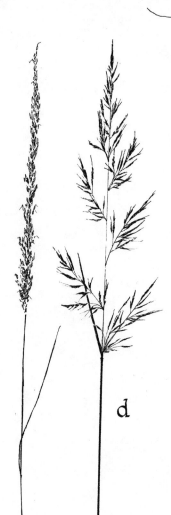

— a

b

Indian Grass
Sorghastrum nutans

Grass family   Gramineae

a small twisted bristles on the
flowers
b slightly fuzzy
c before and after flowering
(closed)
d during flowering (open)
inflorescence is tall and
narrow; golden brown; shining

tall: 60 cm–2.7 m (2–9 ft.)
native
perennial
late summer: August–September

Could be confused with
Arrhenatherum elatius (preceding).
Arrhenatherum is mainly visible
in the spring, has no fuzz, and
ranges in color from green to
purple to silver, never tan.

A striking native perennial,
Sorghastrum nutans is one of the
dominant species of the tall-grass
prairie. In the East it is not
common, but you find it growing
sporadically along dry roadsides
and in fields, often along with
Andropogon gerardi (p. 110). It is
very nutritious for livestock.

d

c

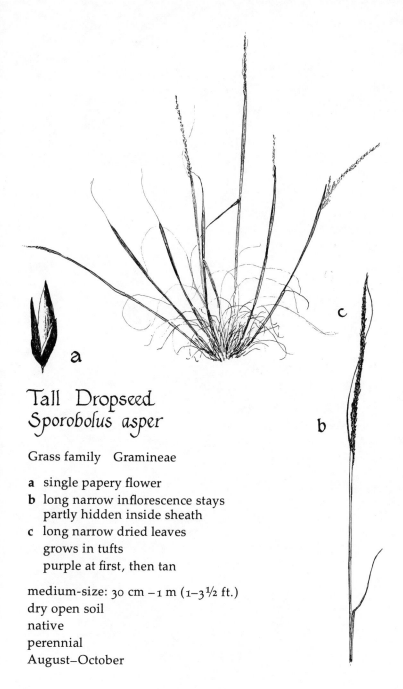

Tall Dropseed
Sporobolus asper

Grass family   Gramineae

a single papery flower
b long narrow inflorescence stays
   partly hidden inside sheath
c long narrow dried leaves
   grows in tufts
   purple at first, then tan

medium-size: 30 cm – 1 m (1–3½ ft.)
dry open soil
native
perennial
August–October

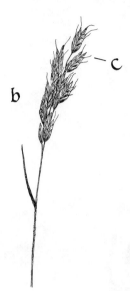

Soft Chess
Bromus mollis

Grass family Gramineae

a leaf sheaths fuzzy
b flower clusters fuzzy, plump
c bristle on each flower scale
   compact inflorescence; branches point
   upward

small: 10–90 cm (4 in.–3 ft.)
grows in small tufts in waste places,
along roadsides, and in agricultural fields
alien
annual

Poverty Grass
Sporobolus vaginiflorus

Grass family   Gramineae

a inflorescence stays tucked inside sheath
grows in scraggly tufts
when dry, often has alternating patches of light and dark on
stem
shallow root system; easy to pull up

low to ground: 20–75 cm (8 in.–2½ ft.)
sterile soil (roadsides, parking lots, and so forth)
native
annual
fall: August–October

Similar to *Triplasis purpurea* (next) which has purple flower
clusters and branches extending farther out from the sheaths.
The tufts are less dense, and *Triplasis* grows more often on
sand beaches rather than in disturbed man-made habitats.
Aristida dichotoma (p. 98) has little horizontal bristles on the
flowers.

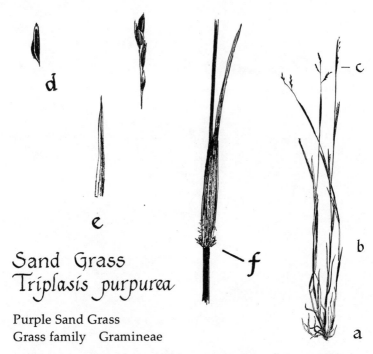

Sand Grass
Triplasis purpurea

Purple Sand Grass
Grass family   Gramineae

a grows in small clumps; lower part of stem sometimes sprawls
b stems stiff, conspicuously jointed, often have alternating sections of light and dark
c flower branches short, often stay tucked inside leaves
d flower scales purple
e short stiff leaves
f little tufts of white hairs at the bottom of the leaf sheaths

10 cm–1.2 m (4 in.–4 ft.)
sand; mainly on the coast, but also inland (a predictable beach grass)
native
annual
fall: August–October

Similar to *Sporobolus vaginiflorus* (preceding) which has green to tan flower scales and grows more often in waste places.

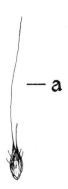

— a

b

Salt · marsh Cockspur
Echinochloa walteri

(*Echinos* means "sea urchin" in Greek, referring to the bristles)

Grass family   Gramineae

a long fine bristles
b dense arching inflorescence, usually purple
c stiff hairs on sheath

tall: up to 2.4 m (8 ft.)
brackish, alkaline, and freshwater shores and marshes
does not grow north of New Hampshire
native
annual

Could be confused with *E. crusgalli* (next) which has shorter bristles, is generally smaller, and does not grow in the same habitat.

— c

Barnyard Grass
Echinochloa crusgalli

a

Grass family   Gramineae

a fat oval flower has short bristles on the outer scales and a
bristle of variable length at the end
green or reddish-purple when flowering
stem often red-purple at base

10 cm–1 m (4 in.–3½ ft.)
waste ground, cultivated fields
alien; grows almost all over the world
annual
June–November

Although Barnyard Grass is generally considered a
troublesome weed, it has a few illustrious relatives. *E.
colonum*, Jungle Rice (not related to true Rice — *Oryza sativa*),
is cultivated in warm countries for fodder. *E. frumentacea*,
from eastern Asia, is also grown for fodder. It was introduced
into this country by enthusiastic promoters and somehow
given the absurd name of Billion-Dollar Grass.

Northern Dropseed
Sporobolus heterolepis

Grass family   Gramineae

a papery blackish scales
b big round seed enclosed in scales
c thin branches
inflorescence purple to black,
6.2–30 cm (2½–12 in.)
grows in bunches with wiry basal
leaves

45 cm–1 m (1½–3½ ft.)
prairies, rocky soil; found only
occasionally in the eastern states,
more common in the Midwest
native
perennial
August–October

a

Manna Grass
Glyceria obtusa

Grass family   Gramineae

a plump flower cluster
b branches all point upward
c dense inflorescence

15 cm–1.4 m (6 in.–4½ ft.)
wet places
native
perennial
July–September

b

c

Wild Rice
Zizania aquatica

Water Oats
Grass family   Gramineae

inflorescence is big, bright yellow-green
when ripe; branches stay after flowers
have fallen off
a very wide leaves
b thin branches in bunches
c female flowers hug branches; fall off easily
d male flowers droop down, straw-color
to purplish
e single female flower
f cluster of male flowers

very tall: up to 3 m (10 ft.)
quiet waters, fresh to brackish
river mouths, marshes
native
annual

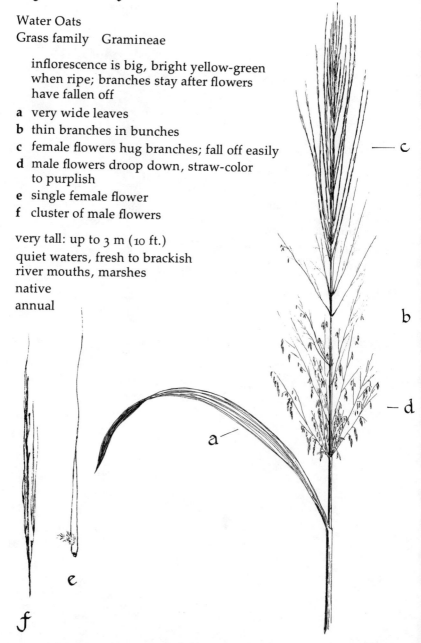

Wild Rice is not related to White Rice (*Oryza sativa*) except by virtue of being a member of the Grass family. Wild Rice, *Zizania aquatica*, is considered quite a delicacy and sells for more per pound than filet mignon in New York delicatessens. Most of what is sold in the U.S. comes from Minnesota, with a little from Canada and Wisconsin. Wild Rice is an important industry for the Chippewa Indians, who are licensed by the state.

Ricing is not an easy operation. If you find some Wild Rice and pick it, you will notice that the seeds fall off almost as you touch it. This is called "shattering." The easy shattering of Wild Rice means that it must be harvested at precisely the right time or the seeds will have fallen off and floated away.

The rice is collected by two people in a canoe, one paddling, the other knocking the plants with a stick so that the ripe seeds fall into the boat. The grains ripen unevenly on the plant so the knocker must be able to apply just the right pressure or unripe seeds will be knocked off, too. It is often said that Wild Rice remains wild, and this is true. So far the plant has resisted attempts to make it conform to efficient modern agricultural techniques. Scientists have tried unsuccessfully to develop a nonshattering variety. Wild Rice has also been grown experimentally in paddies that are drained at harvesting time. The plants are then harvested with a combine. The machine harvest is much more efficient than the canoe method, but not enough seed is left to start a crop for the next year.

Besides being popular with humans, Wild Rice is well liked by ducks and geese, and it is often planted to provide food for them. Although it grows in the greatest abundance in the northern Great Lake states, you can find it here and there throughout the Northeast.

a —

c

Smooth Brome
Bromus inermis

Hungarian Brome   **b**
Grass family   Gramineae

a very short bristle at end of flower
   scale (unlike other species of
   Bromus, which have long bristles)
b single flower cluster, often tinged
   with bronze or purple
c branches point slightly upward

3.8 cm –1 m (1½ in.–3½ ft.)
roadsides and fields
alien
perennial
May–June

Could be confused with *Festuca elatior* (p. 197) which has
shorter, wider flower clusters and scales.

   Bromus inermis was first cultivated in Hungary and
introduced into this country by way of California in 1884. It is
now grown as a forage grass in almost half the country. It is
cold-tolerant and does well in the northern Great Plains with
irrigation.

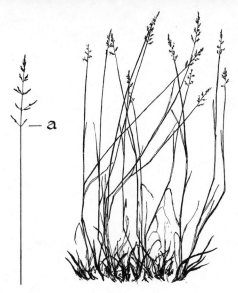

Canada Bluegrass
Poa compressa

(*compressa* means "flattened")

Grass family   Gramineae

a short branches, usually in twos
   blue-green stem and leaves
   try to roll the stem between your fingers; it will not roll
   because the stem is flat

small: 10–75 cm (4 in.–2½ ft.)
grows in clumps in dry soil; it is quite an opportunist and you
can often find it on the only piece of dry soil around, for
instance, on a rock in the middle of a swamp or coming out of
chinks of a wall
alien
perennial
flowers mainly in the spring although the dried stalks persist
through the summer

Could be confused with *Poa pratensis* (following) but is
distinguished by its flat stem, blue-green color, and smaller
size.

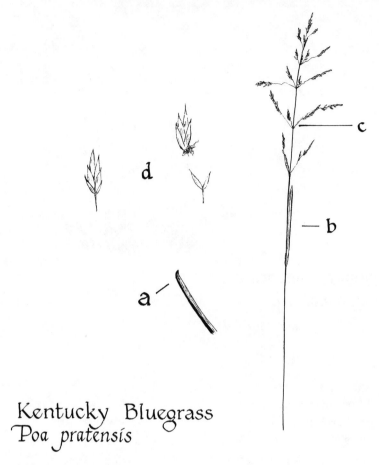

Kentucky Bluegrass
Poa pratensis

Speargrass, Junegrass
Grass family   Gramineae

a boat-shaped leaf tip (characteristic of all species of *Poa*)
b short leaves
c branches in bunches of 3–5
d whole flower cluster; remove bottom two scales and you
will see small tufts of cobwebby hairs at base of remaining
scales
flowers green, then tan
usually grows in patches; spreads by stolons
inflorescence sometimes open, sometimes closed

5–75 cm (2 in.–2½ ft.)
fields, roadsides, lawns, shores; very common
perennial
flowers mainly in the spring

Easily confused with *Agrostis alba* (p. 152) which is usually
purple or brown in flower (rarely green), and shiny. *Agrostis*
only has one flower in each cluster and does not have several
overlapping scales. *Festuca* spp. (see p. 197) have flower scales
that are more pointed at the tip and the plants are generally
coarser. Also, no other genus has the boat-shaped leaf tips
(See next page)

nor the cobwebby hairs at the base of the flower scales. *Poa compressa* is similar but has a flat stem (see p. 191).

Poa pratensis, or Kentucky Bluegrass, is an important grass in our landscape and economy. It is one of the most widely used lawn grasses and is also widely planted as a pasture grass. It is not native to Kentucky. As far as anyone can figure out, the species is native to the northern part of this continent, but was also brought over by European settlers. As a grass of northern origin, it is what is known as a cool-season species—it makes its best growth in the spring and the fall, and is essentially dormant during the summer. *Poa pratensis* spreads by stolons and forms a dense sod (good for lawns) but has a shallow root system and thus needs a reliable source of moisture. One of the most noticeable features of its growth requirements is a marked preference for limestone soils. Kentucky is underlain by limestone (which is why it has its famous caves — limestone is very porous and easily dissolved by water) and has plentiful year-round rain. Therefore, *Poa pratensis* grows well there, whence the name Kentucky Bluegrass.

On the prairie, *P. pratensis* has been an active invader when native grasses are overgrazed, and it has also been planted as a pasture grass. It competes well against the native grasses because it is an "increaser" — a species that grows better after being grazed — unlike most of the prairie species which are "decreasers." Furthermore, many prairie species such as the *Andropogons* are warm-season grasses, which do not grow actively till summer. Therefore, *Poa* gets a headstart on these species and shades them out. However, especially on the mixed-grass and short-grass prairies, rainfall is irregular and *Poa,* with its shallow root system, cannot withstand a drought. The native prairie grasses have deep roots that can reach the water in the lower soil layers. Thus, in a dry spell, the native grasses can regain their position of dominance.

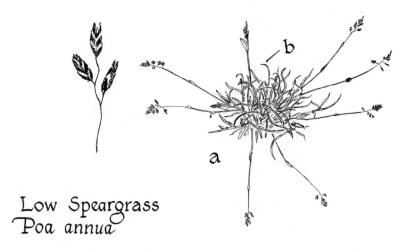

Low Speargrass
Poa annua

Annual Bluegrass, Six-weeks Grass
Grass family   Gramineae

a tufted
b boat-shaped leaf tips (characteristic of all species of *Poa*)

can grow as high as 50 cm (20 in.) but is usually much smaller
dooryards, driveways, waste ground, and clearings
native
annual

This grass is so tiny you could easily walk right past it. It
appears very early in the spring and sometimes again in the
fall. You can find it flowering as late as December. It cannot
tolerate hot weather, though, and usually disappears in the
summer.

Fowl Meadow Grass
Poa palustris
(*palustris* means "of marshes")

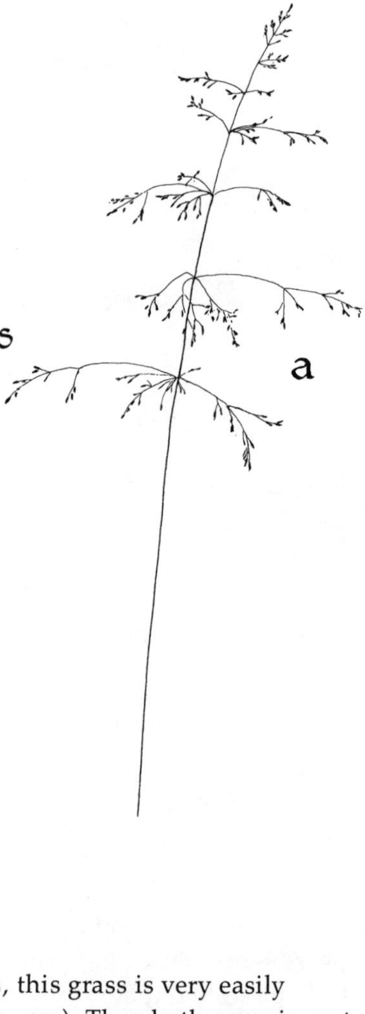

Grass family   Gramineae

a delicate branches in bunches
b single flower; cobwebby hairs at base
flowers green, bronze, or purple at flowering time, then turn tan

up to 1.5 m (5 ft.)
wet places
native
perennial
late June–early September

As the common name indicates, this grass is very easily confused with *Glyceria striata* (p. 140). They both grow in wet places and look quite similar, especially after flowering. To tell them apart, you must look closely at the flower clusters. At the base of each flower scale of *Poa palustris* are tufts of cobwebby hairs, not present in *Glyceria*. The veins are more noticeable on the scales of *Glyceria* flowers.

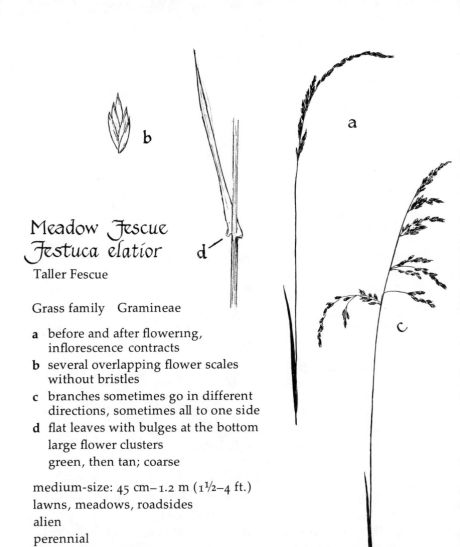

Meadow Jescue
Festuca elatior
Taller Fescue

Grass family   Gramineae

a before and after flowering,
inflorescence contracts
b several overlapping flower scales
without bristles
c branches sometimes go in different
directions, sometimes all to one side
d flat leaves with bulges at the bottom
large flower clusters
green, then tan; coarse

medium-size: 45 cm–1.2 m (1½–4 ft.)
lawns, meadows, roadsides
alien
perennial
June–August
An important forage grass.

Easily confused with *Festuca rubra* (p. 172) which has long
bristles on each flower scale and narrow wiry leaves; no bulge
at base of leaves. *Bromus inermis* (p. 190) has longer flower
clusters tinged with bronze or purple; flower scales usually
have short bristles at end and are widest toward the top.

Stink Grass
Eragrostis megastachya
E. poaeoides

Skunk Grass
Grass family   Gramineae

a grows in small tufts, with stems bent at the base
b short stiff branches
c lead-colored flower scales

small to medium-size: 20–90 cm (8 in.–3 ft.)
waste ground and roadsides
alien
annual; easy to pull up

Could be confused with *Poa pratensis* (p. 191). *Poa* flower
clusters are wider and not as strongly flattened. At the base of
each *Poa* flower scale is a tuft of hairs. *Poa* leaves have a boat-
shaped tip, unlike those of *Eragrostis*.

   Eragrostis poaeoides and *E. megastachya* are very similar.
E. megastachya tends to be bigger than *E. poaeoides* and to
have a more crowded inflorescence. Fresh *E. megastachya*
plants smell bad if you crush them.

   The Latin name *Eragrostis* comes from the Greek *Eros*, the
god of love, and *agrostis*, grass. A concoction made from
Eragrostis megastachya was thought to act as a love potion.

199

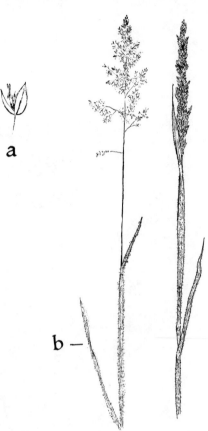

a

b —

Velvet Grass
Holcus lanatus

Grass family   Gramineae

a single papery flower, almost transparent
b gray-green velvety leaves
inflorescence is wispy, pale green to purple
grows in tufts

medium-size: 30 cm–1 m (1–3½ ft.)
fields and waste places
alien
perennial
flowers in spring (May–July), then withers away

No other grass in our area has this velvety texture.

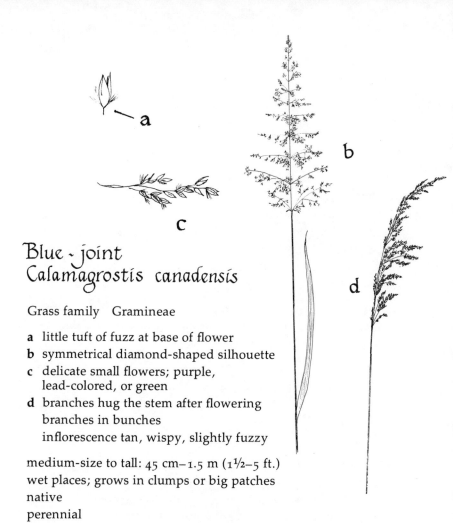

Blue - joint
Calamagrostis canadensis

Grass family   Gramineae

a little tuft of fuzz at base of flower
b symmetrical diamond-shaped silhouette
c delicate small flowers; purple,
   lead-colored, or green
d branches hug the stem after flowering
   branches in bunches
   inflorescence tan, wispy, slightly fuzzy

medium-size to tall: 45 cm–1.5 m (1½–5 ft.)
wet places; grows in clumps or big patches
native
perennial

Easily confused with *Agrostis alba* (p. 152) which has no fuzz
on the flower scales and is usually smaller. *Cinna* spp. (next)
grow in woods and have no fuzz on the flower scales.

   Not very distinctive by itself, but easily recognizable in a
big patch, this grass is very common in northern bogs and
swamps, where it covers large areas. The dried flower stalks
remain for a while after flowering and overtop the leaves.
This was an important, though not very successful, forage
species in colonial times.

Wood Reedgrass
Cinna latifolia
C. arundinacea

Grass family   Gramineae

    pale green to pale purple, then tan
    many branches; usually spreading or drooping
    big inflorescence: 10–40 cm (4–16 in.)

medium-size: 45 cm–1.5 m (1½-5 ft.)
grows in woods in the fall
native
perennial
July–October

Some species of *Festuca* (pp. 172 and 197) are similar but have bigger, coarser flowers; do not grow in the woods.
Calamagrostis (preceding) is a deeper purple; has only a single flower in each cluster; does not grow in the woods.
    Cinna arundinacea has a denser inflorescence than *latifolia* with branches sometimes pointing up. It is much larger.

Oats
Avena sativa
(*sativa* means "cultivated")

Grass family   Gramineae

a two big scales
b big flowers that hang down

30–75 cm (1–2½ ft.)
fields, waste places
alien
annual

This is the cultivated species of Oats used to make oatmeal.
However, most of the commercial Oat crop is grown for
animal feed, and world production has decreased somewhat
since machinery replaced horses. Oats are a recent crop
compared to Wheat and others. They are grown almost
exclusively in Europe and temperate North America.

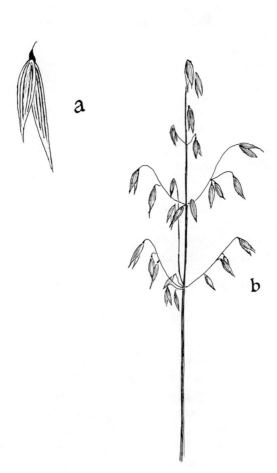

Corn
Zea mays

Maize
Grass family   Gramineae

a wide leaves
b fat stem
c male flowers (tassels)
d female flowers (the "silk" is the styles; each kernel is an individual fruit, in a cluster known as the "ear")

native
annual
occasionally spontaneous in fields and roadsides

A native American crop, Corn was a staple of the diet of most American Indians. Corn needs a certain amount of heat and humidity and it grows best in the part of the United States that used to be the tall-grass prairie (see pp. 8,10). The United States is the leading Corn producer of the world and we feed 90% of our crop to livestock. The development of hybrid Corn, which produces fantastically high yields, was one of the significant developments of modern agriculture.

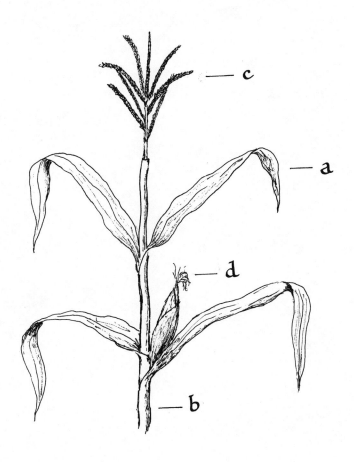

Glossary for Text

alien — not native.

annual — having a one-year life cycle. Annual plants generally have shallow root systems and produce many seeds.

biennial — having a two-year life cycle. In the first year the plant forms a cluster of basal leaves and a large taproot. In the second year it produces a flowering shoot.

brackish water — water containing salt, but in a lower concentration than sea water.

bract — a leaflike or bristly structure under the inflorescence.

bunch grass — a grass that produces many side shoots and thus grows in a clump, as opposed to a sod-former. Some grass species grow either as bunch grasses or sod-formers depending on environmental conditions.

forage — food for domestic animals; fodder.

flower cluster — a small group of flowers, usually at the end of a stalk (technically known as a spikelet), made up of the flower scales (technically known as glumes, lemmas, and paleas). See p. 224 for further explanation of these terms. In the grasses and sedges, the flowers are small and have no showy petals, only stamens (male, pollen-bearing) and pistils (female, fruit-producing). The stamens and pistils are enclosed by the flower scales.

hay — grass and other plants, usually legumes, that have been cut and dried; used for winter food for animals.

inflorescence — the arrangement of the flowers on the stem; the entire assemblage of flowers.

legume — a plant in the Leguminosae or Pea family. Many legumes can "fix" atmospheric nitrogen into a form that is usable by plants. They therefore have high concentrations of nitrogen in their own tissues, and thus make valuable animal food since nitrogen is the essential building block for protein. The increased availability of nitrogen caused by the presence of legumes stimulates the growth of adjoining plants. For this reason, legumes such as alfalfa and clovers are planted in pastures along with grass.

meadow — a grassland that is grown for hay.

pasture — a fenced grassland.

    tame pasture — a pasture that has been planted, usually with a mixture of legumes and native or introduced grasses.

perennial — having a life cycle of several years. Perennial plants usually have large root systems and many do not flower until after a few years.

perfect — of a flower; having both male and female parts on the same flower, as opposed to unisexual flowers.

range — unfenced, uncultivated grassland.

saline — salty.

sheath — the lower part of the leaf that wraps around the stem (see p. 226 for further explanation).

silage — feed for animals prepared by storing green plants — grass and legumes — in a silo, which is airtight. The green plants rot to a certain stage and then, because of lack of oxygen, fermentation can proceed no farther.

sod-former — a grass that spreads by rhizomes and forms a dense mat of roots.

tussock — a big clump of earth usually bound together densely by roots of grasses and sedges.

weed — a plant growing where it is not wanted. Loosely, a species that invades and grows in disturbed areas, or one that spreads quickly. No plant species is genetically a weed.

Habitat Key

"Habitat" means "it dwells" in Latin. In old natural histories, which were all written in Latin, "habitat" was the first word in descriptions of plant and animal species. The English word habitat means essentially the same thing — the kind of place in which a plant or animal usually occurs. Most plants are fairly particular about their habitat and quite predictable. If you go to a certain kind of place in a certain part of the country, you can expect to find certain species.

Therefore I have prepared this listing to simplify your search for a grass name — look for the habitat where you found the plant and then go through that list. This key will be most useful for specialized habitats that support a narrow range of species, such as salt marshes and sand dunes. The key is far from infallible because it is hard to define all habitats exactly and they often grade into each other. Also, be careful when you are collecting to note the habitat precisely. For instance, a roadside ditch will have wet-site species, not roadside plants, and a bare rock sticking up in the middle of a swamp will have dry-site species, not wet.

Fields and Grassy Roadsides; Lawns

Agropyron repens
Agrostis spp.
Allium vineale
Alopecurus spp.
Andropogon spp.
Anthoxanthum odoratum
Arrhenatherum elatius
Bromus inermis
Bromus japonicus
Bromus mollis
Carex lanuginosa
Carex scoparia
Cynodon dactylon
Cyperus esculentus
Cyperus strigosus
Dactylis glomerata
Digitaria sanguinalis
Echinochloa crusgalli
Eleusine indica
Elymus canadensis
Eragrostis megastachya
Festuca elatior
Festuca rubra
Holcus lanatus

Hordeum spp.
Juncus bufonius
Juncus marginatus
Juncus tenuis
Leptoloma cognatum
Lolium perenne
Luzula multiflora
Miscanthus sinensis
Muhlenbergia schreberi
Phalaris arundinacea
Phleum pratense
Plantago spp.
Poa annua
Poa compressa
Poa pratensis
Secale cereale
Setaria spp.
Sorghastrum nutans
Sporobolus vaginiflorus
Triodia flava
Tripsacum dactyloides
Triticum aestivum
Zea mays

Waste Ground: Vacant Lots, Bare Embankments, Parking Lots, Cleared Stripped Land, City Sidewalks (sterile, compacted soil; lots of sun and heat)

Most of these are annuals, species that germinate and flower in a short period of time. As the site becomes more covered with vegetation, there is no space for the annuals to germinate. The plants that succeed the annuals are perennials, which have deeper root systems. The perennials can therefore compete successfully for the available moisture.

Equisetum hyemale
Eriophorum spp.

Typha latifolia
Zizania aquatica

BRACKISH SHORES AND WATERS

Cladium mariscoides
Cyperus diandrus
Cyperus rivularis
Echinochloa walteri
Scirpus americanus

Scirpus fluviatilis
Scirpus robustus
Spartina cynosuroides
Zizania aquatica

SALT MARSHES AND THEIR EDGES

Distichlis spicata
Elymus virginicus
Hierochloë odorata
Juncus gerardi
Panicum virgatum

Phragmites communis
Scirpus americanus
Scirpus robustus
Spartina spp.
Tripsacum dactyloides

WOODS AND SHADED ROADSIDES

Agrostis perennans
Brachyelytrum erectum
Bromus ciliatus
Carex laxiflora
Carex pensylvanica
Carex scoparia

Cinna spp.
Hystrix patula
Juncus tenuis
Luzula multiflora
Oryzopsis asperifolia

Flowering Times

Grasses are seasonal just like other flowering plants. They follow definite timetables, and a May or September landscape will include certain grasses just the way it will include certain wildflowers. It is hard to assign absolute limits to flowering times because of variations in latitude and altitude. Furthermore, for grasses, flowering time is perhaps not as useful an indicator as for showy wildflowers, because many grasses persist in essentially the same form after they have finished flowering. In the fall you might find a grass that actually flowered in the summer, but the ripe stamens and stigmas are usually obvious enough so that you can tell if the plant is really in flower or not. I have not listed here all the species in this book — only the extremes, the very early flowering species and the very late ones.

EARLY SPRING-FLOWERING SPECIES (before May, while the leaves are still coming out on the trees)

Agrostis hyemalis   *Luzula multiflora*
Carex pensylvanica   *Oryzopsis asperifolia*
Hierochloë odorata   *Poa annua*

Fall-Flowering Species (after August)

The richness of fall-flowering is one of the factors that makes grasses a joy to study. Some of the most glorious native grasses stay hidden till fall, when the landscape gets a whole new lease on life.

Agrostis perennans
Andropogon spp.
Aristida spp.
Cinna spp.
Miscanthus sinensis
Muhlenbergia schreberi
Poa annua

Scirpus cyperinus (in fruit, its most conspicuous stage)
Sorghastrum nutans
Sporobolus spp.
Triodia flava
Triplasis purpurea

Very Tall Plants—over 2 m (7 ft.)

Miscanthus sinensis
Phragmites communis
Scirpus validus
Sorghastrum nutans
Spartina alterniflora

Spartina pectinata
Tripsacum dactyloides
Typha spp.
Zizania aquatica

If You Do Not Find Something in This Book

This book only describes the more common or conspicuous species in the northeastern United States. It does not include alpine plants. If you are observant and spend a lot of time outdoors, you will probably start finding species not described here and will need to consult other books. This section will give you some suggestions on books to use and the equipment and techniques you will need to use them successfully.

Books

First, you should try *Field Guide to the Grasses, Sedges and Rushes of the United States,* by Edward Knobel, a 1977 Dover reprint of a book written in 1899. The species selection in Knobel's book is slightly more extensive than in this one and the identification system is simple. Knobel's book is not comprehensive either, however, so your next step is a technical botany manual. To identify grasses (not sedges or rushes), you should begin by consulting the *First Book of Grasses* by Agnes Chase (New York: Macmillan Company, 1922). This not an identification manual but a clear explanation of the flower structure of different grasses. It is an immense help in interpreting the keys.

The following are some of the manuals you might consult. They all have dichotomous keys, the use of which is explained in their introductory sections. If you do not know how to use a dichotomous key, be sure to read the instructions. All the keys are based on flower characteristics and do not differ significantly from each other, but you will probably develop your own preference.

Gray's Manual of Botany. M. L. Fernald, 8th ed., 1950. D. Van Nostrand Company, 1 vol., 1632 pp. Geographical range: the northeastern United States and adjacent Canada, extending westward to Minnesota, eastern Nebraska and Kansas, south to Virginia. Few illustrations.

The New Britton & Brown Illustrated Flora of the Northeastern United States & Adjacent Canada. Henry A. Gleason, 1968. Hafner Publishing Company, 3 vols., 595 pp. Every species illustrated with line drawings. Geographical range: the Northeast and adjacent Canada, only slightly less restricted than *Gray's Manual.* The grasses, sedges, and rushes are all in the first volume, so if you can somehow manage to buy only that, you can save some money. Dover publications has brought out an earlier edition of the book in paperback. The main drawback of this edition is that some of the scientific names are out-of-date.

Manual of the Grasses of the United States. A. S. Hitchcock, 2nd ed. revised by Agnes Chase, 1950. Dover Publications, 2 vols., 1051 pp.; many illustrations. This is the classic, written and revised by two of America's most prominent agrostologists. The only problem with its usefulness for a beginner is that it describes grasses over the entire country. Thus you have many more species to choose from and consequently many more opportunities to make mistakes.

In general, the more you can narrow down your range of choices, the easier it will be to make identifications. To this end, you might want to use a local or state flora. If a good flora does not exist for your state, a flora for an adjoining state will probably serve just as well. Go to the nearest college or university library and look in the section in the stacks under the Library of Congress call number QK 117. Browse around and see what you prefer. Two state floras that have particularly profuse illustrations are *The Illustrated Flora of Illinois* series by Robert Mohlenbrock and *The Flora of West Virginia* by P. D. Strausbaugh and Earl Core. For much of the Northeast, the state floras are surprisingly interchangeable, unless you are concerned with localized habitats such as a salt marsh, coastal beach, or a northern bog.

Another way to narrow down your choices is to find a book written for a certain habitat. These are a few that include grasses, sedges, and rushes:

A Beachcomber's Botany. Loren C. Petry. Old Greenwich, Conn: Chatham Press, 1975.

Tidal Marshes of Connecticut: A Primer of Wetland Plants. Mervin F. Roberts. Reprint Series No. 1. Available from Connecticut Arboretum, Connecticut College, New London, Connecticut 06320.

Mountain Flowers of New England. Appalachian Mountain Club, 5 Joy Street, Boston, Massachusetts, 1964.

If you want to identify grasses in their vegetative state, without flowering shoots, consult these books:

Vascular Plants of the Pacific Northwest. C. Leo Hitchcock and Arthur Cronquist. Seattle: University of Washington Press, 1969.

Some Grasses of the Northeast. A key to their identification by vegetative characters. C. E. Phillips. Field Manual No. 2, July 1962. University of Delaware Agricultural Experiment Station. Newark, Delaware.

Proturf Guide to the Identification of Grasses. Jim Converse. Available from O. M. Scott and Sons, Marysville, Ohio 43040.

Equipment

You will need a 10x hand lens, which you can get at a stationery store, some very fine-pointed tweezers, a razor blade, and a metric ruler with clear millimeter markings. It is also helpful to have a piece of black paper to put the flowers on while you are looking at them. Since most grasses are light colored, the contrast against the black makes it easier to see the distinctive features.

Collecting Specimens

This kind of identification work is not easy to do in the field. It makes more sense to collect plants and bring them indoors for identification. It is essential to collect a good specimen, which unfortunately means the whole plant — roots and all. The keys often separate species on the basis of their underground parts or basal-leaf characteristics. If you are sensitive about pulling up plants, then you should take note of these characteristics in the field. Measure the width of the basal leaves, notice the color and texture and make some drawings. Use your judgment about collecting. If you are looking at a common roadside species, go ahead and collect it. But if the species seems rare, or if you are in an unusual or endangered habitat, such as the New England mountains, don't collect.

In the field you should notice the general growth form of the plant — whether it is growing in a dense clump or whether the stems are separate; whether the plant creeps along the ground or whether it grows upright. Notice also characteristics that might change after picking, such as whether the flowering branches are drooping or upright, and whether the leaves are flat or folded on the edges. Crush the plant and smell it. Try to find specimens in different stages of the life cycle — flowering and fruiting — and try to get typical plants. If possible, collect more than one specimen of each species. Notice the habitat and locality where you found the plant.

One way to collect the plant is to press it immediately, but it is cumbersome to carry a plant press around and you sometimes lose distinctive characteristics in pressing. Another good way to carry specimens in the field is in a plastic bag, tightly tied at the top. If you can't work on the plants as soon as you get home, put the bag in the refrigerator.

Time of Year

Most grasses are best identified when they are in flower, but for some you need the fruiting stage. You might be afraid that grass flowers are so small that you won't notice when they are in flower, but this does not usually matter. It is important mainly to identify the plant before it starts falling apart. For most grass species, you probably have at least a month during which the flower structures stay intact.

For sedges and rushes, you need ripe fruit for identification. What this means, with the exception of a few early spring woodland sedges (like *Carex pensylvanica*), is WAIT. If you try to identify the plants when they are too young, you will only meet with frustration. Fortunately, once the fruit is ripe, most of these plants stay intact for the rest of the season. Most of the sedges are ready by midsummer; most rushes not till late summer or fall.

Explanation of Some Terms Found in Technical Manuals

In a dichotomous key, the decisions are not always easy, and the terminology not always clear. It is beyond the scope of this book to interpret every key word by word, but I hope that the following diagrams and definitions will be helpful. Every technical manual has a glossary of its own, which you should use. I have not included here terms that are easily defined in other glossaries. I have only tried to explain some of the terms peculiar to the grasses, sedges, and rushes that might be confusing. These are not arranged alphabetically but grouped by the part of the plant in which they appear.

FLOWERS

spikelet — a grouping of grass or sedge flowers arranged in a spike. (A spike is an elongated cluster of flowers with no stalks.) In the Grass family, the spikelet is defined by the presence of two **glumes** at its base. A grass spikelet may have just one flower or it may have several.

glumes — two empty scales at the base of the spikelet. The glumes may take many shapes and forms. A few genera (*Zizania, Leersia*) have no glumes; *Lolium* has only one.

lemma — a scale that encloses a single flower. Inside the lemma you will find another scale, the **palea,** and the flower parts (stamens, ovary, and so forth).

palea — a scale inside the lemma that encloses the flower parts. The palea is usually smaller than the lemma and is sometimes hard to see because it may be folded inside the lemma. Some species of *Agrostis* and *Alopecurus* have no palea.

fertile lemma — a lemma with a functional flower inside it, either pistillate or staminate. If you find any flower parts at all, or if you find a grain, you can consider a lemma fertile.

sterile lemma — a lemma with no functional flower inside. Most noticeable in *Panicum, Echinochloa,* and related genera. Sometimes the sterile lemma is so small it may be overlooked (as in *Phalaris*) or so large that it may be mistaken for a fertile one.

floret — flower.

perigynium (pl. perigynia) — in the genus *Carex;* a sac that encloses the female flower.

inflorescence — the arrangement of the flowers on the stem *or* the whole cluster of flowers. There are many types of inflorescences, and the terminology is the same as for other flowering plants. A few of the terms follow.

head — a short crowded cluster of flowers with no stalks.

spike — an elongated cluster of flowers with no stalks (Timothy, p. 84). Many grass inflorescences that look like spikes actually have branches if you pull them apart and are **panicles** (*Ammophila, Alopecurus*).

spikelet — a small spike; *see also* the definition on opposite page.

raceme — an elongated flower cluster with flowers borne singly, each one on a stalk.

panicle — a compound raceme; an arrangement in which the flowers are borne on stalks that branch off larger stalks.

umbel — an arrangement in which the flower stalks radiate from one point at the top of the stem.

rachilla — the axis of the spikelet.

rachis — the axis of the whole inflorescence.

pedicel — a stalk that supports a single spikelet.

bract — a leaflike structure underneath a flower.

bracteole — a little bract.

prophyll — a bracteole at the base of an individual flower.

involucre — an assemblage of bracts under the inflorescence.

sessile — having no stalks.

disarticulation — the point where the flower falls off the plant, usually either above or below the glumes. This happens naturally when the fruit is ripe and ready to be dispersed, but if you wait till this stage to identify the plant, there will be nothing left. To determine the point of disarticulation before the fruit is ripe, take firm hold of a lemma with tweezers. Be sure you are not holding the glumes. Pull the lemma(s) and see if the glumes come with it. If they do, disarticulation is below the glumes; if they do not, it is above. Try this several times to make sure you are right. Sometimes the inflorescence will come apart as you handle the plant (*Hordeum jubatum*) or it will fall off all in one piece. In these cases, disarticulation is either in a group of spikelets, or below the whole inflorescence. You will also see the word **articulation**. Articulation is the point of attachment while disarticulation is the point of detachment; for the purposes of keying out a plant, these are the same.

dimorphic — literally, having two forms; not being uniform. "Spikelets dimorphic" can mean that some are male, some female; some fertile, some sterile; or simply that they are different from each other in some way.

FRUITS

achene — a small hard dry fruit that looks like a seed. The fruit of the Sedge family is an achene.

grain — a small seedlike fruit that is fused to the seed. The fruit of the Grass family is a grain.

capsule — a dry fruit that opens into more than one section. The fruit of the Rush family is a three-parted capsule.

LEAVES AND STEMS

blade — the part of the leaf that extends out from the stem.

sheath — the part of the leaf that wraps around the stem. It is important to distinguish the sheath from the stem, for the sheath could be fuzzy, for instance, while the stem is not, and making the wrong determination could get you the wrong answer in the key.

ligule — a little projection at the top of the leaf sheath, on the inside.

auricle — a lobe or appendage sometimes found at the base of the leaf blade.

culm — stem.

node — the point where the leaf joins the stem, at the base of the sheath.

internode — the space between two nodes.

septate — divided into sections (applies to leaves of certain rushes).

rhizome — a horizontal underground stem that produces roots and shoots at the nodes.

stolon — a horizontal aboveground stem that produces roots and shoots at the nodes.

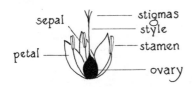

in flower

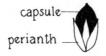

capsule

perianth

capsule opens into three sections

in fruit   ripe fruit

The stamens are still present, tucked underneath the sepals and petals. The three sepals and three petals are similar and are collectively called the *perianth*.

septate

leaf

This characteristic is not always easy to see and shows up better after the plants are dried.

RUSH FAMILY (JUNCACEAE)

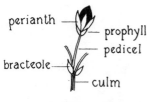

perianth

prophyll

pedicel

bracteole

culm

prophyllate flower

eprophyllate flower

When looking for the prophylls, be careful not to confuse them with the little bracts at the base of the petiole.

227

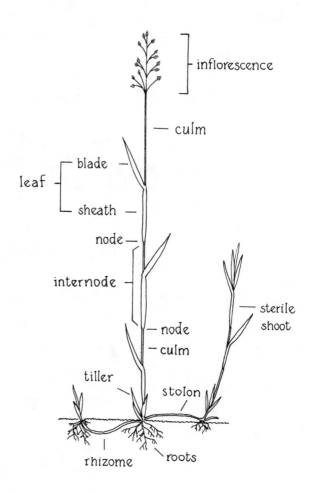

inflorescence

culm

leaf — blade —

sheath —

node —

internode

node

culm

sterile shoot

tiller

stolon

rhizome — roots

GRASS FAMILY (GRAMINEAE)

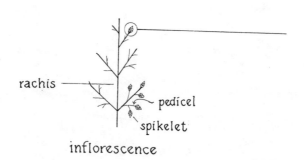

rachis —

pedicel

spikelet

inflorescence

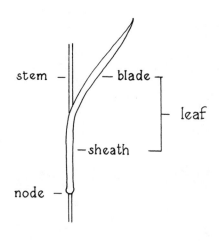

stem —   — blade ⌐

                          ├ leaf

           —sheath ⌐

node —

— blade
— ligule
— sheath

— auricle

the ligule may have different shapes,
be hairy or be absent

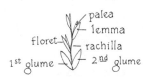

— palea
— lemma
floret — rachilla
1st glume — 2nd glume

a generalized
spikelet

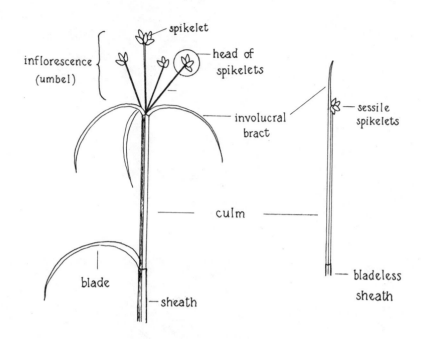

spikelet

head of
spikelets

inflorescence
(umbel)

involucral
bract

sessile
spikelets

culm

blade

bladeless
sheath

sheath

SEDGE FAMILY (CYPERACEAE)

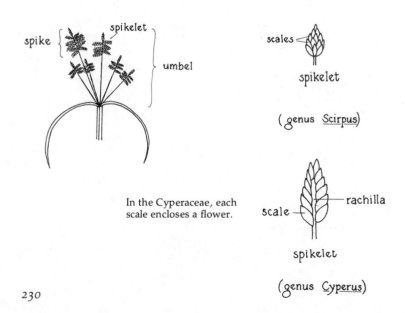

spike

spikelet

umbel

scales

spikelet

(genus _Scirpus_)

In the Cyperaceae, each
scale encloses a flower.

scale

rachilla

spikelet

(genus _Cyperus_)

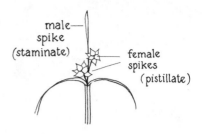

male—
spike
(staminate)

female
spikes
(pistillate)

dimorphic spikes

(some ♂, some ♀)

female
flowers
on top

male
flowers
below

uniform spikes

On plants like this, it can be hard to tell which flowers are male
and which are female. If you find the plant in flower, you will
see the stamens, but the flowering state is too early to key the
plant. If you find it in fruit, generally scales that have perigynia
and achenes inside them are female, and empty ones are male.

the genus <u>Carex</u> family Cyperaceae

The genus *Carex* is distinguished by having unisexual flowers
and by the presence of the *perigynium,* a sac that encloses the
female flower. The perigynium varies greatly in form.

scale   perigynium with flower inside

beak

inflated   flat & scaly

perigynia

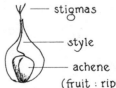

stigmas

style

achene
(fruit : ripened
ovary)

231

Additional Readings on Grasses and Grasslands

This list does not include identification manuals; for those see pp. 220. This list is by no means comprehensive.

Allen, Durward L. *The Life of Prairies and Plains.* Our Living World of Nature Series. New York: McGraw-Hill Book Company, 1967. 232 pp. Discusses animal life as well as plant life, history and ecology. Easy reading.

Gleason, Henry A. and Cronquist, Arthur. *The Natural Geography of Plants.* New York: Columbia University Press, 1964. 420 pp. See Chapter 22, "The Vegetation of North America," as well as the rest. A good introduction to the subject of plant geography.

Pasture and Range Plants. Phillips Petroleum Company, 1963. 176 pp. Available from Phillips Petroleum Company, Bartlesville, Oklahoma, 74004. Fine illustrations of various grasses and forbs, with interesting notes on the use and management of each one.

Teal, John and Mildred. *Life and Death of a Salt Marsh.* New York: Ballantine Books, 1969. 274 pp.

United States Department of Agriculture. *Grass. The Yearbook of Agriculture.* Washington, D.C.: 1948. 892 pp. This book is made up of many short essays on all aspects of grass usage.

Watts, May Theilgard. *Reading the Landscape. An Adventure in Ecology.* New York: Macmillan Publishing Company, 1957. 230 pp. See Chapter 2, "Prairie Plowing Match."

Weaver, J. E. *Prairie Plants and Their Environment. A Fifty-year Study in the Midwest.* Lincoln: University of Nebraska Press, 1968. 276 pp. An easily readable collection of an ecologist's observations. Studies of root systems, plant competition, and changes over time.

Wilder, Laura Ingalls. *Little House on the Prairie.* New York: Harper and Row Publishers, 1935. 335 pp. For children and adults; part of an autobiographical series.

Index to Species

Primary common names are given in **boldface;** alternate common names are also listed. For more information about nomenclature see pp. 18–19.